BOOMERS OUT OF THE BOX

Other books by Paul H. Lutton:

Plan B: The Economic Development of the Eastern Region of Puerto Rico Through the Decolonization of Vieques, available at www.lulu.com

The Vieques Renaissance Supplemental Discussion Guide, available at www.vieques-libre.com/essays/

BOOMERS OUT OF THE BOX

BOOMERS OUT OF THE BOX

BOOMERS OUT OF THE BOX

Single Seniors' Guide to Out-of-the-Box Thinking and Online Dating

By
Paul H. Lutton
With
A Lot of Help from My Friends

BOOMERS OUT OF THE BOX

Figure 1. Boomer stuck in the box.

BOOMERS OUT OF THE BOX
is published by Paul H. Lutton

ISBN: 978-1-7376410-6-3

© Copyright 2024 by Paul H. Lutton
Contact paul@boomers-out-of-the-box.com

www.boomers-out-of-the-box.com

TABLE OF CONTENTS

DEDICATION xv
PREFACE: WHY THIS BOOK? 19
INTRODUCTION: MAKING THE MOST OF OUR SENIOR YEARS 23
PART 1: TRANSFORMATION 29
CHAPTER 1: LIFE, IT IS A CHANGING 31
   CHANGES IN ATTITUDE: ADAPTING TO NEW REALITIES 31
   SO, WHAT'S CHANGE GOT TO DO WITH IT? 33
      Risk and Reward 35
      Balance 37
   DEALING WITH LOSS: REAL LIFE STORIES 38
      My Story 38
      Susan's Story 39
CHAPTER 2: WHO DO WE WANT TO BE? 41
   A STORY OF EMBRACING A TOTAL LIFE CHANGE 44
PART 2: RELATIONSHIPS & DATING 47
CHAPTER 3: SOCIALIZATION 49
CHAPTER 4: ABOUT RELATIONSHIPS 53
   TYPICAL RELATIONSHIP TYPES 54
      Friendships 54
      Companionships 54
      Friends with Benefits (FWB) 54
      Close Friends with Benefits 55
      Monogamous Romantic Partnerships 55
      Marriage 55
      Open Relationship 55
      Polyamory 55

- Swingers 56
- Hookups 56
- Situationships 56
- DIY 56
- Something for Everyone 56
- What Fits Your Intentions? 57
- IS NOW THE TIME FOR A NEW RELATIONSHIP? 59
- CONSIDERATIONS 60
  - Logistics & Time Commitments 60
  - Personal Assets & Traits 61
- FORMULATING THE GOAL 65
  - Jennifer & Carlos 66

CHAPTER 5: MODERN DATING 69
- BABY BOOMER DATING PARADIGM 70
- OTHER DATING PARADIGMS 72
  - Gen X 72
  - Millennials 72
  - Gen Z 73
  - In General 73
- WHAT ABOUT US, NOW? 74
  - Becoming Active 74
  - Our Own Backyards 75
  - Speed Dating 75
  - Power Up the Internet 76
  - Getting Ready 78

CHAPTER 6: ONLINE DATING PROCESS 81
- PHASE 1: THE CANDY STORE 82
- PHASE 2: ELECTRONIC CONTACT 83
- PHASE 3: THE FIRST DATE IS A MEET-AND-GREET 84

PHASE 4: REAL DATING 85
PHASE 5: EXCLUSIVE DATING 86
MY STORY – OF COURSE IT IS UNIQUE 87
CHAPTER 7: WHO ARE WE NOW? 95
  ARE WE READY FOR A NEW COMMITMENT OR
  RELATIONSHIP? 95
    Legal & Financial 96
    Physical Condition 96
    Mental & Emotional States 96
    Other Issues 97
CHAPTER 8: CREATING A PLAN FOR ACTION 101
  SETTING OUR EXPECTATIONS 102
    Reflections from Barbara 108
  IMPLEMENTING THE PLAN 109
    Getting Started Online 109
    Will AI Be Able to Help? 112
CHAPTER 9: THE PROFILE 115
  CONSIDERATIONS FOR THE PROFILE 117
    Relationship(s) 117
    Time & Distance 117
    Personal Traits 117
    Preferences 118
    Background, History, &.... 120
    Religion & Politics 120
    Physical Appearance 121
  CREATING THE PROFILE 122
  MESSAGING 126
    Traditional & Chance In-Person Meetings 129
    My Personal Experience with Filtering 129
CHAPTER 10: SECURITY 131

- SAFE DATING 131
  - Scams 131
  - Red Flags 131
  - Rules 132
- SAFE TECH 134

CHAPTER 11: FORMAL DATING 137
- GET READY, 'CAUSE HERE IT COMES 137
  - Expectations for the Meet-and-Greet 138
  - Where to Meet? 138
  - Personal Presentation 138
  - Dating is not a Reality Show 144

CHAPTER 12: BUILDING RELATIONSHIPS 147
- AS TIME GOES BY 148
  - Developing a New Perspective 149
  - Coming Clean – Avoiding a Future Disaster 150
- PERSONALITY 152
  - Personal Traits 153
  - Social 155
  - Relationships 155
- RECOGNIZING OUR DIFFERENCES 158
- COMPROMISE 160
- EMOTIONAL INTELLIGENCE 161
- COMMUNICATIONS 163
  - Confirmed Dialogue 163
  - Understanding 165
  - Feedback 165
- INTIMACY 168

PART: 3 SEX & AGING 171

CHAPTER 13: SEX & THE MODERN SENIOR 173

REALITIES OF SENIOR SEX 174
SEXUAL EXPLORATION & COMMUNICATION............. 179
   Sexual Subjects to Discuss 179
   Detailed Feedback 181
   Experimentation 182
CHAPTER 14: SEX PHYSIOLOGY 101 187
THE BRAIN IS THE CONTROL CENTER......................... 188
EROGENOUS ZONES & SEXUAL PLEASURE 191
NON-GENITAL EROGENOUS AREA STIMULATION 194
   Head Area 194
   Extremities... 194
   Torso Plus 195
GENITAL DESCRIPTION & FEMALE BIT STIMULATION
.... 198
   Cunnilingus Techniques 201
   Female Ejaculation 203
   Squirting 203
   Edging 204
GENITAL DESCRIPTION & MALE BIT STIMULATION .. 205
   Fellatio Techniques 207
   Oral Sex 209
   Sixty-Nine 210
   Anal Play 210
ORGASM: AN EXPERIENCE OF CLIMAX IN SEXUAL
PLEASURE 212
   Who Knew?.. 212
   Satisfaction.. 215
CHAPTER 15: SAFETY 217
SAFE SEX 217
   Venereal Diseases 217

    Anal Intercourse 218
    Choking During Sex... 220
    Recreational Drugs 221
    225
PART 4: LIVE LONG AND PROSPER 226
CHAPTER 16: GO FORTH AND LIVE THE LIFE YOU TRULY WANT 227
    HAPPINESS 228
        Contentment & Satisfaction 228
        How's it going now?.. 229
        Fun, Fun, Fun... 230
        Tomorrow 231
        Putting It All Together 231
    A LOVING RELATIONSHIP'S GOOD FOR YOU 232
    DO IT AGAIN, BETTER 233
    IN CLOSING 237
ACKNOWLEDGEMENTS 239
REFERENCES 241
LIST OF FIGURES 247
USEFUL LINKS 251
ABOUT THE AUTHOR 255

BOOMERS OUT OF THE BOX

DEDICATION

This book is dedicated to those who have been fortunate enough to be part of the wackiest and most wonderful generation that ever existed. We're not the Greatest Generation, that distinction belongs to our parents. Without their heroic efforts and sacrifices, our lives, had we even been created, would have been quite different.

While we Boomers haven't, for the most part, had to fight for survival, our less tenuous existence has given us the opportunity to work on refining and elevating societal norms. We have been active participants in the efforts to right wrongs, to seek peace, to provide more equality for everyone, and to party on.

BOOMERS OUT OF THE BOX

Figure 2. Getting out of the box.

BOOMERS OUT OF THE BOX

PREFACE: WHY THIS BOOK?

Facing the prospect of dating in this phase of our lives can be daunting. While I have been pursuing my long-term goal of finding the woman I want to spend the rest of my life with, I have acquired an appreciation for the journey and enjoyment from meeting potential partners. In fact, during the process of performing the research, listening to interviewees, and structuring discussions to encourage Boomers to think out-of-the-box, I have learned a tremendous amount and come to the surprising conclusion that my own thinking has been unnecessarily constrained, and I have more to learn and new options to explore.

I owe a great deal to the incredible women whom I have had the good fortune to date over the last five years. Those experiences highlighted the fact that, despite a 39-year marriage and a subsequent 12-year relationship, there was a void in my understanding of personal relationships that needed to be addressed. While I never before sensed anything was missing in my personal development, I came to realize I was wrong, and it was time to "go back to school".

I have researched senior-oriented dating books, podcasts, articles, webinars, etc., and I have interviewed other seniors to learn more from both sides of heterosexual relationships in the hopes of becoming better prepared to navigate the dating world and date with purpose. I wanted to develop the skills needed to present myself more effectively and to determine which prospects were likely to end up being compatible matches. I wanted to learn how to build and maintain a healthy, lasting relationship. In the process, I have gained insight into life and relationship building that has made me a better person and a better partner. I finally understand and appreciate emotional intelligence and have become more empathetic to the feelings and emotions of others.

Reminiscing, I recalled an event from about 30 years ago. I attended a one-man show in a large theater in Chicago

BOOMERS OUT OF THE BOX

entitled "Men Are from Mars, Women Are from Venus". It was absolutely hysterical and deemed accurate, unanimously, according to all of the heads in the audience nodding together. We all laughed, went out to dinner, and in a short time forgot about it. I should have bought John Gray's book by the same name; and kept it next to the bed; and read it over and over again.

Since beginning online dating in 2019, I have seen many excellent profiles and photographs, but they were the exceptions, not the rule. The majority were ineffective, and many were dismal. It has been disappointing to receive profiles of prospects who may have been good fits, but because their presentations were so lacking, I deleted them. Now it's easy to say, "That's their loss." and move on, but it's also my loss if they were someone with whom a meaningful relationship could have developed.

My experiences got me thinking. Retired from my various careers, could I dedicate some time to help coach seniors who are afraid of entering the dating game or struggling with the dating process? What value might I offer to fellow seniors? Based on my research and experience, I determined that I could help in several ways:

First, and foremost, by encouraging "out-of-the-box" thinking and planning. It is deceptively easy to follow the traditional paths of our elders that are no longer relevant or optimal for us in our current world. New opportunities, technologies, social norms, and unprecedented longevity demand a fresh look at life as a senior. Change is reality, and we need to have open minds if we are to be prepared to make the best of our golden years.

Second, by authoring this book. While this volume provides coverage of important aging issues, its focus is aimed at encouraging open-mindedness, embracing change, catalyzing successful socialization through dating, and building relationships. It is intended as an overview or a guide rather than a deep dive.

Third, by creating a website for seniors. www.boomers-out-of-the-box.com is broader in scope and deeper in areas of

PREFACE

socialization and sexuality than I could include in this book. www.boomers-out-of-the-box.com includes links to websites curated by professionals offering a large range of coverage in pertinent specialty areas of interest to seniors.

Ultimately, it is up to each of us to reinvent ourselves as we see fit and find a match (or matches) to share happiness and joy for this phase of our lives. We can then create a lasting relationship to meet our needs. This book is offered as an aid to that end. People are unique and situations are diverse, so there is no single solution that fits us all. Please keep an open mind to the infinite possibilities and opportunities. Remember, this is a guide, not a bible. Do not be afraid to blaze your own trail to find YOUR way.

Please note that I would love to hear about your experiences in senior dating either before or after reading this book at: paul@boomers-out-of-the-box.com

BOOMERS OUT OF THE BOX

INTRODUCTION: MAKING THE MOST OF OUR SENIOR YEARS

People are living longer than they used to. After reaching 65 years old, average males can expect to live to 83 and females to 85. That is roughly 20 years and represents **almost a third of our adult lives.** Those in good health can expect a higher quality of life and even greater longevity than the overall average. So, let's not squander the significant and precious time we have left acting as though the game is over. There are so many ways to make our golden years fun and productive, and even if we are experiencing these joys already, we might still want to examine different possibilities, set thoughtful goals, and pursue new dreams.

As we move through the many phases of our lives, changes in our minds, bodies, social relationships, and curtailed activities present themselves as new challenges to address. Historically, society has adopted the mindset that those of retirement age are through with the serious world, and they are relegated to playing golf, endlessly watching TV, or just waiting alone for the grim reaper. These stereotypes belie both the reality and the opportunities available to seniors today.

Our task begins with self-reflection to affirm who we are and determine who we want to become. The opportunity for change at this point is manifest. By reviewing our histories honestly and considering our strengths and our weaknesses, our skills and our deficits, our assets and our liabilities, and other factors we can shape what our preferences for change may be. This can lead us to deciding whether to attempt to reinvent ourselves or continue on our current paths.

BOOMERS OUT OF THE BOX

The modern senior is busily engaged in a range of activities including childcare for their grandchildren, volunteer work[1], starting new businesses, pursuing hobbies, traveling, enrolling in online and traditional school courses, participating in physical fitness programs, and a million other things. Social engagement is a critical component of healthy aging as well, and most of the following chapters address elements of socialization with a focus on preparing for dating and second chances.

Part 1 looks at the transformation that has taken place in the world of technology, societal norms, aging, and opportunities for senior living.

Chapter 1 directly addresses the issues of change that depart from our expectations and historical patterns. It exposes the tradeoffs of risks and rewards and reminds us to maintain a life balance.

Chapter 2 confronts us with the question, "Who do we want to be?" Facing the many life changes being presented to us, whether we like them or not, how do we live the rest of our lives? We have the power to reinvent ourselves, but are we ready to embrace a life change?

Part 2 is about relationships and dating, both of which have changed significantly over the last decades.

Chapter 3 reinforces the importance of socialization to avoid isolation. Health and longevity suffer greatly in the throes of loneliness.

Chapter 4 jumps into defining the array of relationships that are common and available to us. The list is much longer than we might imagine, and it is worth our time to investigate and consider options that we would never have contemplated before. Upon gaining an understanding of the opportunities that might satisfy our intentions and desires, we can confirm

---

[1] Volunteer opportunities abound. AmeriCorps Seniors alone facilitates the placement of about 143,000 seniors in community service opportunities every year, according to a Washington Post article by Javier Jaen. https://www.washingtonpost.com/opinions/2024/12/02/seniors-service-americorps/

INTRODUCTION

our readiness to seek and prepare for a new relationship. Next, we can define the goals that will guide us through the planning process that follows.

Chapter 5 presents the generational evolution of dating from WWII until the present. As we will see, there has been a sea change over the years, and this chapter gets us up to speed.

Chapter 6 reviews the five phases of online dating titled:

1. The Candy Store
2. Electronic Contact
3. The First Date is a Meet-and-Greet
4. Real Dating
5. Exclusive Dating

This is followed up with my personal online dating story.

Chapter 7 assists us in defining who we are and helps us to determine our readiness for a new relationship by examining the state of our affairs – from legal issues to mental, physical, and emotional conditions. In this chapter, we also address the loss of loved ones and dealing with grief.

In Chapter 8 we formulate a plan. First, we work on setting realistic expectations. Next, we tackle the task of presenting ourselves in an honest and effective way to attract as many prospects with the desired attributes as possible while dismissing as many mismatches as possible at the same time.

Chapter 9 is all about creating our online profiles. This includes some dos and don'ts as well as some specific examples.

Chapter 10 addresses safe dating as it relates to avoiding scams, recognizing red flags, and setting/following rules and boundaries. It also covers a few tech recommendations.

Chapter 11 is the dating chapter. It addresses issues relating to expectations, the first meeting, personal presentation, and more.

Chapter 12 covers a lot of ground in relationship building. It looks at developing new perspectives in coupling and avoiding

BOOMERS OUT OF THE BOX

a common disaster. It offers us the criteria to evaluate our personalities and their inherent compatibilities with the personalities of a potential match. In this chapter, we also discuss compromise, emotional intelligence, and communications.

Part 3 examines the many facets of sex and aging.

Chapter 13 begins with the realities of our aging bodies as well as the potential accommodations we can (or must) make to provide and receive the most pleasure and satisfaction in our relationships. It offers encouragement to replace expired limitations from our past experiences with a healthy exploration of more enlightened opportunities for sexual expression. Thorough communication is critical to achieving sexual pleasure, and immediate feedback plays a very important role.

Chapter 14 offers sex education basics through a shallow dive into physiology which presents the body parts engaged in sexual functions and their roles. Discussions of erogenous zones, love making techniques, sexual pleasure, orgasm, and intimacy inform the senior with a sufficient depth of knowledge to engage confidently with purpose in sexual activities.

Chapter 15 examines safety in the form of safe sex. Venereal diseases are growing faster in seniors than in other age groups. Anal sex, choking, and recreational drugs can present unexpected dangers that are reviewed.

Part 4 focuses on parting instructions to aid in proceeding forward and leading a happy life as a senior.

Chapter 16 talks about happiness, contentment, satisfaction, and having fun. It also offers encouragement to continue these efforts in the face of rejections and other obstacles. These stumbling blocks do not proclaim failure, they just mean: "Okay, do it again better this time."

There are roughly 20 million living members of the Silent Generation (born between 1928 and 1945) and 75 million Boomers (1946-1964) in the US. We have shocked and annoyed the establishment since day one. We have questioned authority and refused to play by the rules. We

INTRODUCTION

have rebelled against traditional gender roles, brought marijuana into the mainstream, and revolutionized sexual norms. So why stop now? As seniors, we may feel invisible to younger people, but do we really want to go quietly into the night? Nobody is looking at us, so let's break out of the box – again! Why not? Let's go out on fire. Let's do stuff.

Note that, due to my service as an Air Force pilot, I use many quotations and examples from my military origins. And from my years in a garage band, my other favorite source of inspiration is the poetry from my favorite songs.

BOOMERS OUT OF THE BOX

PART 1: TRANSFORMATION

Figure 3. Transition: one foot on the platform, and one foot on the train.

BOOMERS OUT OF THE BOX

CHAPTER 1: LIFE, IT IS A CHANGING

"Change can be viewed as either exciting or frightening, but regardless of how we view it, we must all face the fact that change is the very nature of life."
By Michael A. Singer, <u>The Untethered Soul</u> [1.1]

CHANGES IN ATTITUDE: ADAPTING TO NEW REALITIES

There is another major change or paradigm shift taking place in the process of aging that many haven't realized or acknowledged: we're not our parents' or grandparents' embodiment of old. Being elderly **ain't what it used to be**. When we consider how our elders aged, it is not necessarily a valid road map for us. Many of our generation are refusing to behave as if they are over the hill. We are staying fit, engaged in physical activity, aware of current events, exercising our minds (formally in classes and on our own), dating, having sex, and seeking new lifestyles. We are not acting as if getting older is the end of the line but are enjoying a new-found **freedom from expired responsibilities.** We are pursuing activities that are pleasurable and exciting as we gain greater self-awareness and wisdom. We are intent on remaining relevant.

By the time we have reached retirement age, our decades of experiences have formed a solid picture of our worlds both big and small. It is certainly true that most of the knowledge we have gained over our lifetimes is practical and factual. We know that if we stick our bare hands into a fire, we are going to get burned. If we step in front of a fast-moving truck, we are likely to become roadkill. We also "know" things that we believe are facts, but are they accurate? Were they true once but no longer true or relevant?

BOOMERS OUT OF THE BOX

I did not eat broccoli for decades because I did not like it as a kid. A few years ago, I tried some, and I discovered that it was surprisingly good. The government had convinced most of us that marijuana was addictive and would lead us to heroin. But time has proven that it is less damaging than cigarettes or the heavy use of aspirin. In science class we learned there were 9 planets, but astrophysicists defrocked Pluto as a fake. Many churches preach that sex between unmarried couples is immoral, and when we were much younger, many of us agreed, even if we violated the "rule" ourselves. Many of us now appear to strongly disagree. *Over 90% of adults have had sex before or outside of marriage.*

We have traditionally viewed grandparents as background dependents soon to be cared for like children. We are often invisible in groups of mixed ages. Many believe seniors should sit back, enjoy the peace and quiet, and be free of meaningful responsibilities until they "*die, and they lay them to rest*"[2]. Clearly some retired, disabled, or unhealthy folks are too tired or infirm to continue life with the same intensity, energy, or capabilities. But too many wrongly feel that they are in a phase of terminal maturation: time to merely rest and live out their lives with menial activities. Is this the time to **open our minds** to the opportunities at hand? Is this the time for an attitude check: Are we stuck with all sorts of beliefs, rules, and incorrect perceptions that make us rigid and unyielding involving both major and even minor issues? I'd say this is the time to adopt the attitude of "can do" and to **reevaluate** the importance of the conflicting views of the past and present.

---

[2] From the song "Spirit in the Sky" by Norman Greenbaum.

CHAPTER 1: LIFE, IT IS A CHANGING

SO, WHAT'S CHANGE GOT TO DO WITH IT?

Change has everything to do with life. Change is the inevitable result of the passage of time. External changes impact us, and the changes we make impact the world in small, and even sometimes, in larger ways.

Change seems to affect everything and be everywhere like never before, especially as we age. But truthfully, rapid change was constant when we were children as well. In our youth, we looked forward to getting bigger, stronger, older, and more privileged. As we matured, many of us began to dread changes in routines, responsibilities, and in our bodies. We worried about legal, policy, and administrative changes altering our attempts at academic achievement, employment, and career progression. As societal norms evolved, we became anxious over social acceptance, political correctness, gender roles, and dating success. Some embraced the opportunities that change offered; it stressed others out.

Concern over the unknown is rational, but misplaced fear is not healthy and can overwhelm our emotions and ability to reason clearly. Much change is both natural and unavoidable. We can ignore some changes with denial and confront others with resistance. Or we can accept the inevitability of change, prepare for it, and go with the flow.

We can disregard technological innovations - accepting life in the slow lane. We can sometimes successfully fight proposed legislative and administrative changes to laws, permits, etc. such as preventing fast-food or bar establishments in our neighborhoods. Or when we see changes coming, we can benefit by rapidly adapting to them – such as when streaming began to emerge, we probably wish we had possessed the foresight to sell our CD & DVD collections while they still had value.

Most senior citizens have experienced major changes in their lives, including some, or possibly all, of the following:

BOOMERS OUT OF THE BOX

Education comes with demonstrable changes in daily living and relationships. Whether setting off for kindergarten, first grade, junior high, high school, or college, the new environment will be quite different. When schooling requires living away from home, the changes can be even more extreme.

Careers begin with transitions from school into first jobs or the military and often include relocation. Changing jobs, careers, or military status presents additional challenges. Unemployment and retirement can have a tremendous impact, as can business failures and major financial successes.

Personal lives undergo constant change throughout life's journey from dating to marrying, having children, and possibly divorcing. PTSD from experiencing a natural (or unnatural) disaster first-hand can be debilitating. Coming out into the LGTBQ+ world is life altering.

Disability through injury or illness can totally disrupt one's life whether it's our own or that of a loved one. Even more extreme, the death of a family member or close friend is often devastating.

The challenges of new situations and opportunities allowed (or even forced) us to reinvent ourselves. It is truly a gift that we have this chance to "start over" at the various inflection points of life. It is easy to become very fixed in our ways and hang onto patterns of living that do not suit us at all as we transition from one life situation to another. Maybe this is the time to overcome inertia; quit living our lives through the rearview mirror and evaluate present and near-future prospects.

> *"Oh, God, give us courage to change what must be altered, serenity to accept what cannot be helped, and insight to know the one from the other."*
>
> Attributed to Reinhold Niebuhr

We are not dead yet and may even have decades left above ground. Time is precious, so why not make the most of it? It is not time to give up our dreams because we have reached a certain age. We can still be productive, pursue fun activities, and seek romance with a loving companion.

CHAPTER 1: LIFE, IT IS A CHANGING

We may not have created formal bucket lists, but we probably have much that we'd still really like to do, although we might not yet see a path to its accomplishment. It is often helpful to adopt an attitude that allows us to step out of our cozy shells to do what we really want. If our efforts do not work out, we can either write them off or try again with a different approach. It may be a suitable time to be a bit more self-centered. Let us not allow others' limited vison, lack of approval, or influence to subvert our inner needs or desires. Let us not allow the risk of embarrassment or failure to put a wet blanket over us. We are not living our lives for the pleasure or amusement of others; it is our life to live as we wish. If not now, when?

But rational, intentional change does not come easy for most of us. It requires an open mind. It requires us to reexamine the status quo and consider alternatives. It requires the givens (habits, rules, beliefs....) of the past to be reevaluated for their current applicability. We don't want to be living our lives and limiting our choices by guidelines and constraints that no longer serve us.

Throughout the remaining chapters, a wide range of lifestyles, relationship types, and sexuality options are presented for consideration. These are not necessarily suggestions, but rather introductions to opportunities that you may wish to explore.

Risk and Reward

No discussion of decision-making, nor of contemplating change is complete without an understanding of risk versus reward.

> *"No expansion or evolution can take place without change, and periods of change are not always comfortable. Change involves challenging what is familiar to us and daring to question our traditional needs for safety, comfort, and control."*
>
> By Michael A. Singer, <u>The Untethered Soul</u> [1.2]

Risk is related to the possibility of something bad or unexpected happening. We know that the risk of getting into a fatal accident on a motorcycle is significantly greater than while riding in a car, but there are too many variables (unknowns) to accurately predict the outcome of a specific trip to Home Depot.

When the variables are identifiable, accurate projections are possible. For example, in a casino's double-zero Roulette wheel, there are 18 black, 18 red, and 2 green pockets for a total of 38. The odds of getting black (or red) are statistically predictable: 18 out of 38, or 47.37%. The chance of getting any particular number or specific slot is 1 out of 38, or 2.63%.

There are interesting factors that govern how acceptable a risk is. We might be very willing to put a small sum down to bet on a single number for a 1 in 38 possibility of winning 36 times the amount bet. But would we be willing to bet our lives (or our financial future) for a huge reward if there was a 1 in 38 chance of losing big?

As another example, the fictional series Squid Game had 456 players who were each willing to take the chance of being the one and only survivor to receive $38M. That's a 455/456 (or 99.78%) likelihood of dying. I don't know anyone who would even consider it. But what if the odds were reversed; only one would die, and the others would all receive the reward? That's a .2% risk of dying for a $38M reward. I'm sure many would be willing to take the risk. I'm not one of them.

Most people recognize that there is risk involved in doing something new. What if the plan fails? Could I lose money? Might I get hurt? Will I be embarrassed if the answer is "no"? What the majority fail to realize is that there is also a risk in not changing. A simple example can be seen in the stock market when a stock has risen quite a bit, there is often a reluctance to sell because the stock may still be on the rise. But if we hold tight, there could be a correction that wipes out the profit (or worse) tomorrow. That's the risk of doing nothing. We constantly face decisions that involve risk.

Life-altering decisions are often very difficult to make. In most cases, the risks in deciding to change or follow an opportunity are not fully clear, nor are the chances of obtaining the hoped-for reward. It can feel safer to do nothing. There are times in our lives when we need to be conservative to protect our families financially and emotionally. As we reach retirement, we typically have more financial certainty, available time, fewer commitments, and general flexibility. What we don't have is as much time left on the clock as we would like. Can we afford to squander some of our resources? Are we wasting our remaining years paralyzed by fear of change and indecision?

Balance

Maintaining a life-balance is important in all phases of our lives, but as seniors, we've been through a lot and may not have found staying in balance to be easy with so many demands on our time from work, family, friends, and health to a myriad of other things. As we age, however, the load of our obligations tends to decline, and achieving balance can be less difficult.

There is no magic formula for how much time and resource should be allocated to different activities. Becoming aware of what you are actually doing is a good start. In this way you can invest the appropriate effort to optimize the precious time you have left.

BOOMERS OUT OF THE BOX

DEALING WITH LOSS: REAL LIFE STORIES

"Losing isn't always the end, sometimes it becomes the beginning."

Joseph Duffy

My Story

I have long been an optimistic and happy person who greeted everyone with a smile. I had recently experienced a series of traumatic events and found myself depressed.

It all began in 2017 with a Category 5 hurricane that left our small island community devastated. Infrastructure was destroyed leaving us with no water for weeks and no electricity for months. Our hospital was condemned, the lush vegetation was left denuded and leafless, and wooden homes were destroyed. Volunteering to provide relief and recovery for over a year, I was left with PTSD, as were most residents of the island. Still, I smiled and had hope.

In 2019 I lost my partner of 12 years to cancer and one of my best friends died just two months later. In 2020, I was fortunate to find love online right before the pandemic. I lived with her for eight months, during which time I got colon cancer and had successful surgery. Shortly thereafter, my new-found romance fell apart, and I was invited to move out. Through the sadness, I still managed to muster up a smile.

In 2021, I had another run at dating, and after 3 months, it was sadly over. My smile was resolute, but weak. I began to realize that I was depressed but couldn't figure out specifically why. I had evaluated everything in the past, from my early years up until the present, but I felt that I had reconciled everything, and I was at peace with each issue. I was sure I had visited every significant loss, failure, and event that could have been the cause of my depression, but nothing jumped out. One night it came to me: I was mourning the loss of my youth.

At 75, I could no longer pursue many of the activities I loved in the past. I lost faith that I would find another partner comparable to my dear lost love. It was a shock to discover the cause of my depression, but by identifying the issue, I was able to focus on resolving it. It was necessary to acknowledge the truth and symbolically memorialize it to move on. Life is good! I smile easily again.

Susan's Story

Susan's story is typical of many widows' experiences. She had dated very few men before marrying, and she was numb with grief at 62 when her one-and-only passed. Over the course of 5 years, the pain of loss morphed into a feeling of an unnatural void that cried out to be filled. Becoming a single woman had not impacted her day-to-day activities with girlfriends, but it had severely trimmed her dinner and evening social life that was often couples oriented.

At 67, Susan began to believe life might be more fun and interesting if she could share things with a good man. While the goal was uplifting, the concept of dating was terrifying. She had no idea how or where to begin. Friends set her up with a few widowers and bachelors, but the results weren't very satisfying. Her daughter had been successful at finding romance online and suggested she give it a try.

On her own, Susan stumbled through signing up for Match.com and attempted to build an engaging profile. She was able to create a reasonable presence, but it was taxing and not attracting the men she intended to target. A yoga friend of hers, who had found her partner online, offered to give her some guidance. She recommended a book and several videocasts that helped her present herself in a way that dramatically improved the suitability of her matches.

For ten months, she had been dating and having fun before she met the man she's been with for the last year. During the process, she had to overcome her initial guilt at being "unfaithful" to her late husband, her embarrassment at not knowing how to date, and fear of failure when she was rejected. She also had to reject quite a few matches along the way. She is now an enthusiastic proponent of online dating.

BOOMERS OUT OF THE BOX

CHAPTER 2: WHO DO WE WANT TO BE?

It's too late to invent the wheel or the microprocessor, but now might be a perfect time to reinvent ourselves.

Figure 4. Is it time to change direction? Does happiness and satisfaction seem more likely on the current course or on a new one?

Considering all the changes with which we are steadily bombarded - from technological innovations, governmental regulations, evolution of moral attitudes, and shifting politics, to a whole host of other things of varying importance – we need to ready ourselves to accommodate or respond to new realities. Not everyone will seriously agree to reevaluate and consider making changes, but hopefully you are not among them. So, what kind of changes are we looking at?

BOOMERS OUT OF THE BOX

Before we hit the slopes and begin to cut a trail to our new lives, it would be wise to establish our goals and intentions for this new life. As we begin the process, we must take an honest look at ourselves, our assets, our skills, our hopes, and our dreams. We are further obligated to acknowledge our liabilities and limitations. We need to formulate possible plans for our desired future that are consistent with our capabilities and constraints.

While it is beyond the scope of this book to provide the answers, the intention is to offer useful questions to help you navigate your journey. An inventory of past experiences, such as follows, can help:

- What do you want to take with you, and what do you want to leave behind? Perhaps in the past you have had pets, but they would become a burden with a different lifestyle. Maybe you've been collecting antique furniture that won't fit in a smaller home.

- What activity/activities have you been interested in but were unable to pursue for reasons that are no longer valid? Are they feasible now, and would you like to consider them as an interest, hobby, business, social practice, or volunteer effort? Most likely you were time constrained in your working and child rearing years but are free now to pursue other activities.

- Is now the time to relocate to be closer to family, to seek better weather, to avoid high taxes and the cost of living, to discover a safer simpler life, to find a dating pool of greater depth, or to start a new adventure?

- Does this new chapter of life need to be a linear continuation of your previous one or do you want to explore a new lifestyle? Have you ever thought about running a bed and breakfast, moving to the country, traveling the world, becoming a naturist (nudist), living on a boat, or joining a commune?

- Have you been locked into a role that was begun decades ago and has been impossible to change

CHAPTER 2: WHO DO WE WANT TO BE?

before? Is now the time to start over with a different image and purpose?

- If you can't identify a specific new direction that you are eager to pursue, are you willing to consider following an unknown path that may be chosen by a future partner?

Clearly the ship has sailed on many potential destinations, but a nearly infinite number of possibilities still remain for those of us who have open minds, the desire to envision a different future, and the drive to follow a new path. For those of us seeking new possibilities and willing to reset a bit or reboot our lives, now might be the time - before establishing a partnership with someone based on expired criteria.

Many fear change but want or expect things to get better in some way. Better requires change. Choosing to change requires an open mind to risks: no risk, no reward.

"If not now, when?"

Hillel the Elder

Figure 5. Time for a change. Opening minds may stimulate getting off the paved highway.

43

BOOMERS OUT OF THE BOX

A STORY OF EMBRACING A TOTAL LIFE CHANGE

As I approached 60, employed and living the good life with my kids launched and still married to my childhood sweetheart, I began to get restless. I had been working in construction in Chicago, where the weather suited my clothes but neither my comfort nor my psyche. I longed to establish a design-build business in the tropics with a backdrop of warm water, beaches, and umbrella drinks. Based on numerous vacations to such destinations, I focused my attention on the tiny Caribbean Island of Vieques, Puerto Rico and, over the course of two years, found a financial partner, obtained the required licenses, and acquired our first property to develop. I relocated to the island alone.

Despite studying Spanish for 3 years at the local high school adult education program, my grasp of the language was poor. I did not have a single friend, and my previous social life, which had been curated by my wife, was no longer accessible. I had no clue how business was conducted in this foreign environment and had a lot to learn.

My response was to address each of the issues head-on. I enrolled in a local Spanish class. I went out to dinner every night, which kept me from starving (I was not a cook), and introduced me to many who became close friends. I reached out to local government employees to get a feel for working within the system. After two years I became totally immersed in the community, a committed full-time resident, and a successful builder. I attribute my gratifying transition to several factors.

After realizing that I was at a point in my life where I could make a major change, I determined what I really wanted to do, even though it took a few years to loosen up and explore the options. Eventually, the fantasy side of my brain allowed me to visualize myself on an island paradise. This triggered my practical side to fully investigate the potential opportunities.

CHAPTER 2: WHO DO WE WANT TO BE?

I read extensively and considered the differences between living with a Type A approach versus living in a basic Type B environment. I trusted my gut that a laid-back existence was what I needed and wanted. It was scary, but I figured: "If not now, when?"

A positive attitude in support of change was essential. This was a voluntary decision; I was not being forced into something; I was not running away but moving toward a goal I had set. Furthermore, I knew if my plans did not work out, it wasn't going to kill me, and I could always return to the States.

Leaving my friends and wife behind (she did not want to live in a rural, tropical community) was a heavy price to pay, but it was a setback that I ultimately overcame without regret.

After 19 rewarding years in the Caribbean, I again decided to reinvent myself. My *novia* (girlfriend) of 12 years had passed in 2019, and I deeply missed her and our relationship. The dating pool for a then 73-year-old man on a small island with extremely poor healthcare was non-existent. My kids lived in the States, so I decided to go online to find a woman near them and the grandkids. My story continues as a delightful work in progress.

BOOMERS OUT OF THE BOX

PART 2: RELATIONSHIPS & DATING

Figure 6. Enjoy the journey.

BOOMERS OUT OF THE BOX

CHAPTER 3: SOCIALIZATION

*"It's time to head straight for them hills
It's time to live and have some thrills
Come along and have a ball
A regular free-for-all"*

From "Summertime, Summertime" by The Jamies

Socialization is a significant issue for people of all ages, but seniors, as a group, are more likely to be lonely and/or isolated than other age segments. This can lead to depression, which can then lead to health problems and/or exacerbate existing conditions. Socially active seniors have happier, healthier, and longer lives than those who are not engaged with family and friends. In fact, according to a 2002 study published by the National Library of Medicine, seniors with more positive perceptions of aging added 7.5 to their lifespans over those who did not.

Additionally, according to an article in the Washington Post, a study "...published in the journal Nature Mental Health in October [2024], polled 608,561 individuals... indicated that feeling lonely increased risk for all-cause dementia by 31 percent and cognitive impairment by 15 percent."[3.1]

It is easy to accept the premise that interacting with those whom we like and love is best for us, but it can be difficult for many to accomplish this for an array of reasons. The major purpose of this book is to offer hope and guidance to those who want or need help socializing, getting the most out of their senior years, and attaining a high quality of life.

Some factors often stifle meaningful face-to-face interaction including:

- Grief. Death of friends & family members.
- Relocation. Friends moving to warmer climes or retirement homes.
- Physical distance. Living in remote and rural areas with small populations.

BOOMERS OUT OF THE BOX

- Mobility. Marooned, being unable to travel or get around without assistance.
- Silos. Cloistered in high-rise apartments and condominiums with only elevator social lives.
- Lack of friends or acquaintances with things in common. Living in a neighborhood where there is little to no personal connectivity between ourselves and others in age, ethnicity, culture, language, finances, backgrounds, or interests.
- Personal sociability. Being shy, introverted, depressed, disabled, immobile, or unhealthy.

Retirement offers more time for maintaining relationships and pursuing activities in which we are interested. This can lead us into social scenarios with like-minded people; and that is a wonderful place to start.

Short or long-term dating is a deliberate and direct form of engaging in socialization. It is seldom dull, usually a worthy adventure, and a good first step toward building relationships. And remember, **dating need not be synonymous with romance. Many date for friendship or companionship.**

CHAPTER 3: SOCIALIZATION

Figure 7. Loneliness is common. Socialization is extremely important for senior health.

BOOMERS OUT OF THE BOX

CHAPTER 4: ABOUT RELATIONSHIPS

"The purpose of a relationship is not to have another who might complete you, but to have another with whom you might share your completeness."

Neale Donald Walsch, Author

While we all have had some form of one or more relationships in the past, what are our choices for this phase of our lives? We need to consider the type of relationship as well as the term or practical duration. Statistically, those of us in our mid-sixties have an average of 15 years of life to look forward to. Those in their mid-seventies can expect 10 more years, and those in their mid-eighties, 6 years. Considering that the loss of one partner ends the relationship, it is clear that contemplating the length of a prospective relationship requires lowering our expectations for what may constitute a long-term relationship.

After coming to grips with the longevity issue for our individual ages, the next thing to consider is the type of relationship that fits us best.

TYPICAL RELATIONSHIP TYPES

"Do what you did at the beginning of the relationship and there won't be an end."

Tony Robbins

Friendships

Friendships can be based on common interests and participation in shared activities. A good friendship is one built on caring (romance not required), concern, support, and the joy of being together. Sports, hobbies, clubs, volunteer groups, classes, etc. can foster relationships that expand into other social settings. They can also evolve into more personal, robust, or full-scale intimate relationships. (Note the cinematic popularity of the term "friend-zone" is over-stating the warning that a friendship can never be elevated to become a successful romance. I, and many friends, have become lovers and entered long-term committed relationships with others who began as friends.)

Companionships

Companionships are friendships with more extensive sharing of time, support, and communal activities. Many seniors prefer almost full-time friends. If romance is involved, it could take the form of a romantic partnership.

Friends with Benefits (FWB)

FWB represents a decidedly uncommitted relationship with sex and play as the goal. These F***-Buddy arrangements are typically intended as limited-term, and both parties should be onboard with agreed upon ground rules. From a practical point of view, at the lowest commitment level, they are essentially repeated hookups with or without a schedule. The source for these serial trysts can be the result of an initial hookup, failed dating attempts at a longer-term connection, or other forms of fraternization that include satisfying sex. Typical participants are looking for reliable, safe, easy, and uncomplicated ways to quickly satisfy their sexual desires and get back to their other

CHAPTER 4: ABOUT RELATIONSHIPS

interests. Often, these relationships do not include appearances as a couple, meeting friends and family, traditional dates, overnights, or meaningful affection.

Close Friends with Benefits

This is an emerging solution, similar to FWB, for couples who have close attachments to one another but want less time commitment and a more open arrangement than a partnership would require. This is out-of-the-box problem solving that fits many of the more open-minded of today's seniors. It offers an additional benefit to couples who connect intensely at some levels but are not sufficiently compatible and don't want to live together in a day-to-day environment. This also works well for couples who live far apart or are only available part time.

Monogamous Romantic Partnerships

Romantic partnerships are like marriages without government or religious underwriting. Generally, there is mutual agreement to the arrangement. Cohabitation is common but not necessary.

Marriage

Marriage is a legal agreement to form a new entity. Many feel it is important to invest the time, hassle, and funds required for religious and/or personal reasons. In addition, with the agreement of both parties, other legal constructs can be added, such as prenuptials and postnuptials, to customize the formalities as desired. The older the partners, the less likely marriage will be chosen.

Open Relationship

An open relationship means each partner is allowed to independently have one or more outside sexual partners. It's an arrangement that both parties agree is committed in some form (often a marriage) but is non-exclusive or non-monogamous. The arrangement's agreement terms are key.

Polyamory

A polyamorous relationship is a romantic or sexual relationship with more than one partner together at the same time, with the full consent of all involved. A throuple is a polyamorous relationship among three people who are romantically and intimately involved with each other.

Swingers

Swingers are coupled partners who enjoy consensual non-monogamous sex with other couples, singles, or groups. Sex parties and sex clubs provide venues for interaction. Couples may also initiate sex with other couples they meet.

Hookups

Casual sex through hookup websites like Tinder are generally thought of as the exclusive domain of younger people and the LGBTQ+ community, but seniors are also participating. It's often just sex to satisfy horny people without attachment. Statistics for senior casual sex are not directly available, but trends toward less commitment are rising as evidenced by the significant rise in sexually transmitted diseases in our age cohort.

Situationships

This relationship, unlike the others, is not the intention of the couple but an undesirable result of poor or deceitful communication. Situationships are similar to friends with benefits, but one person has been led to believe it is more committed or involved than it is for the other. The problem that can lead to heartbreak is that one party – knowingly or unknowingly – is essentially stringing the other along. For example, during the dating journey, one partner may lose interest but can't, or doesn't choose to share this.

DIY

The Do-It-Yourself method is a custom design that will bring whatever both parties want to the partnership. We can do it our own way with near total freedom, as long as both parties agree. Nothing is off the table when we think outside the box.

Something for Everyone

Monogamous, polyamorous, swinging, open, or other? For the most part, the majority of us have been indoctrinated to a maintain monogamous lifestyle. Some of us, however, are

CHAPTER 4: ABOUT RELATIONSHIPS

wired differently and choose to pursue less traditional relationships. A subgroup of us has been monogamistic in the past but now is curious about other arrangements and/or has a fear of missing out (FOMO) on something exciting and pleasurable. For those in the FOMO group, since this is a time of reinvention, why not research the options? If you have a willing partner, this could become a couple's adventure and may lead to unexpected pleasure. This is an opportunity for Boomers out-of-the-box thinking! Merely investigating these options can be exciting whether or not there's an ultimate commitment to an alternative lifestyle.

There are many reasons that people will choose hookups, friends with benefits, or other casual sexual relationships. Many are not ready for commitment! Some want more independent living styles but still want sexual relations. There is something for everyone available.

What Fits Your Intentions?

The options are many, but what do you really want from a new relationship? Maybe it doesn't make sense to seek to replace your former relationship with something similar. Maybe exploration of a less formal arrangement makes sense.

For those of us who have only experienced monogamous relationships, we might wish to consider something different for this next phase of our lives. There are several reasons that this break with tradition may fit the situation more perfectly:

We might have believed that finding The One would create a union in which both parties would complete one another and lead to nirvana. Those concluding that this might be fantasy may wish to find missing pieces to wholeness and satisfaction outside of their primary relationship.

When cohabitation is not desired or possible, we may want to live more independently so that we can pursue social activities that interest us but not our partners. Some become very fixed in their ways and less flexible, making cohabitation and the lack of mutual satisfaction problematic.

When work, family, distance, or special interests demand significant time apart, a second relationship could fill the gap.

BOOMERS OUT OF THE BOX

For successful long-term results, it is important that all relationships, whether romantic or Platonic, be consensual and transparent. Evaluate and confirm the type of relationship you wish to pursue.

Every relationship will benefit from periodic reviews. Honest and forthcoming discussions can help tweak or more radically modify any agreements to tailor or optimize the relationship to the changing needs and requirements of each person.

CHAPTER 4: ABOUT RELATIONSHIPS

IS NOW THE TIME FOR A NEW RELATIONSHIP?

As you think about new directions for your life, is a new romantic relationship something you would like to embark upon? Do you feel ready and available to begin a new relationship? Are you willing and able to put forth both the time and effort required?

Have you reviewed the financial, legal, physical, mental, and emotional condition of your life as described in Chapter 2? Are you satisfied with your situation? Would you feel comfortable disclosing any outstanding legal, financial, citizenship, health, etc. issues with a new partner? If not, would it not be better to work on fixing those items that could become a problem before engaging with or attempting to date someone so the relationship is built on trust? Friendships also need to be based on trust, but some issues might not adversely affect someone when there is neither commitment nor romance.

At the end of the day, if you have any serious issues, or multiple smaller items to resolve, are you really ready for a loving relationship? Can you present yourself honestly? If your issues are not correctable, it's important to own them and put them on the table early on. The field of potential matches may become measurably smaller, but it never goes to zero.

CONSIDERATIONS

> *"If you don't know where you're going, any road will get you there"*
>
> Alice in Wonderland

A goal is an objective and serves as a target for achievement. If you are seeking a loving, lasting relationship, you must first define what that means. There are many variables to identify and prioritize. A good place to start is to determine the type of relationship you are looking for and some of the specific qualities in the partner you are searching for.

Logistics & Time Commitments

Time together is a key element that must suit both parties for the relationship to endure. Some of us still have commitments to work, children, grandchildren, parents, organizations, and other activities that require dedicated time. We have differing preferences on how much togetherness we need or want. Likewise, differing amounts of alone time are required or desired by each of us.

Distance apart is an important consideration if you do not envision living together. Travel time and mobility are factors that impact time apart and quality of life. When a significant commute is involved, spontaneity, convenience, and stress levels can suffer.

Habitation is likely to be separate, each with his or her own dwelling, especially in the early stages of a relationship. The upside is that time apart is available to allow decompression as needed. Regular patterns can evolve where certain days are spent together, and other days are spent at the respective homes. The downsides include the commute, the expense of maintaining two residences, and not being able to enjoy having dinner together most nights or coffee together most mornings. Part-time cohabitation can evolve to full-time as the relationship matures. (See L.6 in Useful Links for further in-depth discussion on the topic <u>LATitude: Living Apart Together</u>.)

CHAPTER 4: ABOUT RELATIONSHIPS

"Sometimes I wonder if men and women really suit each other. Perhaps they should live next door and just visit now and then."

Katharine Hepburn

Personal Assets & Traits

The following reviews some of the important attributes you might want to consider in your evaluation of the suitability and compatibility of a prospective match. Keep in mind that the selection process is a two-way street: your attributes need to be sufficient to attract the partner with whom you hope to match as well. You can think of this as both parties making a list of pros and cons regarding each other individually plus both of you combined.

As an example, open, honest, and clear communication is very important in every phase of dating and relationship building. You can rate yourself and the skill of your prospective partner, but you also need to consider the combination.

> *I dated an excellent match for almost a year. I believe that I am a good communicator, and I felt she was skilled as well. But for whatever reason, we constantly failed to communicate accurately, and it frustrated both of us. What appeared to be a pro on the individual level became a significant con the relationship level.*

Confidence, with humility and the absence of arrogance, is a pro and one of the more effective traits to display in attracting others in dating as well as many other areas of life. Others typically feel more comfortable in the presence of such people.

A person's history and accomplishments tell a story that provides insight into the prospect's nature, personality and motivation. If you like and respect the story, that's a huge pro.

Intelligence and education are not always related. Education can be delineated resume style to reflect achievement and interests, and it can also identify common experiences. This can present a pro, but not always.

BOOMERS OUT OF THE BOX

Determining the intelligence of a match requires more interaction in dating activities. People generally expect that others know what they know, but they don't, and that is not necessarily reflecting lesser intelligence. Literature, art, music, entertainment personalities, homecare skills, etc. are often assumed to be common knowledge. This is not always the case; you must not confuse knowledge for intelligence. So, unless you only want to be with someone who is versed in particular areas, it will be important to accept differences and deficits in another's experiences. While educational level might be easy for you to score pro or con, intelligence is a bit trickier if it is important to you.

Interests & hobbies identify potentially common activities and pursuits that reinforce the concept of togetherness. Not all couples need bonding in this way, but some degree of shared interests strengthens the relationship and also helps in the initial stages of dating. This can be a simple pro or con.

Kindness is always an important criterion. Who wants to build a life with an unkind person? However, it can sometimes take a longer period of time to recognize the true nature of the match in this area. This is a very important criterion, so it had better be a pro.

Sensitivity – there are two basic types or meanings of sensitivity in relationships as it relates to this discussion:

- The first is empathy toward others. This requires the ability to feel the range of emotions of another - much as that person feels them. Most are born with the capacity to empathize, but life experiences cause some to become more (or less) empathetic over time. Sensitivity of this type generates understanding which underlies a meaningful and successful relationship. (This is an important quality for both partners to develop. See the section on emotional intelligence in Chapter 12.) Possessing this capacity is an important pro.

- The second is the level of vulnerability of one's own ego to the words or actions of others. Are we thin skinned,

CHAPTER 4: ABOUT RELATIONSHIPS

guarded, or do we take things too seriously? Do we find ourselves questioning why we are so often hurt by others? Are we too sensitive or is it that others are insensitive and not empathetic? Are we confused why some people take everything we do or say personally? Are we insensitive or are these others overly sensitive? It's beneficial and important to figure out which it is. We can't change others' sensitivity, but we certainly can improve our own. An oversensitive ego is likely to be a significant source of friction in a relationship and definitely a con.

Physical attributes are generally visible in photos, and our value judgements follow. While this is normal, beware that in many cases, our personal filters (whether preferences, biases, or prejudices) discard suggested matches with whom we might have been happy had we gotten to know them first.

- When we look at a person through the lens of desirability and compatibility, it is natural to think: "Do I wish to be seen with this person?", "Do I want to kiss and have sex with him or her?", and "What will my friends and associates think?" While height, weight, body shape, and attractiveness may seem superficial, it can be a core element of the animal courtship hierarchy. Own it.

- As we age, we often think of ourselves as being younger than we are, and thus younger people will often be perceived as more suitable and similar to us. That may not be the case.

I dated a couple of women who were 15 or so years younger. Our common histories were uncommon! How could I live with a partner who wasn't familiar with the Everly Brothers or Woodstock?

- Ethnicity, race, and cultural differences add complexity and richness to relationships. We need to keep open minds to the benefits but be realistic as to the challenges.

BOOMERS OUT OF THE BOX

- Fitness has a range of levels from people who are couch potatoes to exercise junkies. What is important to us when it comes to health and fitness?

- Gender is no longer considered binary but has many options including LBGTQ+. The focus of this book is senior socialization and has general coverage applicable to anyone in the age group but does not cover many unique issues related to orientations outside of straight heterosexual.

- Hair styles (including colors) and shaved areas are personal preferences that send a message of who we are or want to be. Our prospective partners may have strong feelings one way or another about hair length, facial hair, pubic hair, and body hair. Some decisions we make (such as a man's moustache or a woman's Brazilian) might be negotiated later, so it can be to everyone's benefit not to let these elements cause an immediate rejection.

- Hygiene can be an issue if someone is unclean in any area, period. This includes **every part of the body** from the toes to the ears, nose, and hair.

- Oral health in the form of dentil appearance is critical to many. Discolored or missing teeth can send a bad vibe.

Politics is so polarizing these days that if either person is overly outspoken or obsessed with it, the game could be over. Rational people can disagree and discuss differences, but most interactions between Tribe Left and Tribe Right are anything but rational. It is possible to live harmoniously if we can agree to disagree and not feel the need to change others' minds or "enlighten" them with our truths. A con here is not a good sign.

CHAPTER 4: ABOUT RELATIONSHIPS

FORMULATING THE GOAL

> *"You can't always get what you want*
> *But if you try sometime you'll find*
> *You get what you need"*
>
> Rolling Stones

Most of us probably subscribe to the intent of the Stones' lyrics, but on-line dating can sometimes present the opposite result. Christian Rudder of OKCupid suggests that with today's technology, it is easier to find what you want, but not necessarily what you need. Think about it.

While we are primarily addressing our desired relationship goals, we need to remember the other important elements of our intended lives that we examined earlier: "Who do we want to be?" Ultimately, our relationship plans must be consistent and compatible with these personal life goals. If we really wish to spend a significant amount of time seeing the world, our goals should include finding a partner who loves to travel.

> *When I first began dating online, I was living on a beach in Puerto Rico. I stated in my profile that my goal was to be in the SF Bay Area one third of the year and on the island the remainder of the year. I was hoping that I could find a match who was willing to live a third of the year (or more) in the Caribbean with me. Many promising women were unwilling to live outside of the Bay Area for any length of time and rejected me based upon my goal. The system worked. Eventually, my situation changed, I moved to the Bay Area, and my goals likewise changed.*

Goal setting is your personal task. Only you can determine what best fits your needs and desires. Take some time and examine your options. How do you want to live the rest of your life? Who do you want to be?

BOOMERS OUT OF THE BOX

In the following story, Jennifer didn't consider all her needs when establishing her goals the first time through.

Jennifer & Carlos

Jennifer and Carlos were in their late seventies and had both recently relocated to the Denver suburbs to be close to their families. Both had thoughtful sets of criteria which outlined what they were looking for in a partner. The two discovered each other online; both found the other interesting, so they met for coffee to get more fully acquainted. All went very well, and they soon had a second date. The chemistry was compelling, and the romance began to blossom.

They lived an hour apart and spent a couple of days each week at one or the other's homes. Because they were new to the area, neither had made any significant friends. Jennifer was a very social person, but Carlos was happy just being with her. After several months, Jennifer realized that creating an active social life with Carlos was not going to happen in an acceptable amount of time, if at all. She concluded that, despite her love for him, their relationship was not sustainable, and she ended it and returned to online dating. This time, she amended her goals to include finding a man with an active social network.

Timing is another component of our goal. We need to decide when we are going to begin and when we hope to have completed our quest. (See setting expectations in Chapter 8). We need to be flexible and recognize that goals can change over time. Seniors have more than their share of injuries, illnesses, and unexpected detours that will interfere with and frustrate progress.

CHAPTER 4: ABOUT RELATIONSHIPS

BOOMERS OUT OF THE BOX

CHAPTER 5: MODERN DATING

Dating as a senior presents a series of challenges, but finding "The One" (or Ones) makes it all worth the effort.

Dating has taken many forms over the decades, influenced by societal, cultural, and technological shifts. This is a broad overview of how dating has changed from the Baby Boomers to Gen Z. But whatever the process and format, the essential purpose is to enable individuals of like minds to get together. The following provides a review of the many opportunities available to incorporate into your plan.

"Dating is different when you get older. You're not as trusting, or as eager to get back out there and expose yourself to someone."

Toni Braxton

Figure 8. Remember the soda fountain.

BABY BOOMER DATING PARADIGM

For Baby Boomers, dating began in elementary or high school. The actual age of first-time daters was dependent upon community norms and the individual schools. Usually, the boy and girl already knew each other. Except for Sadie Hawkins or turnabout dances, the boys asked the girls out. Dates might have started out at a drugstore soda fountain or hamburger joint, places that we could walk to. Destinations like bowling alleys, miniature golf, and movies often required a car, so mothers and older friends with cars were enlisted. Once we reached driving age, the process was still similar, but the destinations changed dramatically to include drive-in movies, lovers' lanes, submarine races[3], parties at out-of-town venues, etc. Most of the cars of the era had bench seats, so the favored activities often went beyond talking.

As boys and girls morphed into young men and women dating became more formalized. After graduating from high school, those who went to college had a semi-established dating pool of other students with whom they shared classes, parties, dances, and events. Those who went into the workforce often lived in the neighborhoods they grew up in, so, in addition to the pool of known local men and women, people from work added more depth to the pool.

Traditional dating rituals, like going steady or getting pinned if in college, were common, and gender roles were more pronounced, with men typically taking the lead in initiating relationships and planning dates. There was less openness about sexuality until the free love movement of the sixties and early seventies and changed everything for a small but highly visible portion of our cohorts.

---

[3] Fiction created by high school kids. We lived near Lake Michigan, and when going to make out in a park that overlooked the lake, we would say that we were going to watch submarine races. I assume all coastal areas had their equivalents.

CHAPTER 5: MODERN DATING

OTHER DATING PARADIGMS

More recent trends in dating that have occurred with younger generations have had an impact on the current norms seniors are experiencing. Things have changed, and it is to our advantage to understand the new opportunities.

Gen X

For the next generation (those born between 1965 and 1980), the dating pattern moved in the direction of hanging out in groups with less emphasis on formalized individual dates in high school. Casual dating became more prevalent, with more focus on exploration and personal freedom.

The rise of technology began to impact dating with the introduction of personal computers and early forms of online dating services like Match.com in 1993. A few years later we saw the beginning of a low-tech, face-to-face activity called speed dating.

A shift in attitudes towards marriage and commitment led to higher divorce rates and more single-parent households. The AIDS crisis in the 1980s led to increased awareness and concern about sexual health.

Millennials

Born between 1981 and 1996, Millennials became the first generation to grow up with the internet and social media. Initially, dating in high school was characterized by hanging out in groups, like Gen X, but morphed into a hookup culture as it became more driven by online sites such as Tinder offering more efficient and direct options in finding potential partners. Casual sex became more prevalent and socially acceptable among young adults. Millennials delayed marriage and prioritized education and career advancement, leading to longer periods of singlehood and cohabitation before marriage.

CHAPTER 5: MODERN DATING

Gen Z

Gen Z is still a work in progress, given that they were born between 1997 and 2012, and their ages are only 13 to 28 in 2025. Technology is more deeply integrated into dating, with apps like Snapchat and Instagram playing significant roles in communication and forming connections. Virtual dating became more common, especially during the COVID-19 pandemic, with video calls and online activities replacing in-person dates.

Gen Z tends to prioritize authenticity and inclusivity in relationships, valuing honesty, and open communication. There is a blurring of traditional gender roles, with more fluidity in sexual orientation and identity.

In General

Overall, dating has become less morally constrained and more diverse, casual, and technology-driven across generations, reflecting broader societal changes in attitudes towards relationships, gender, and sexuality.

BOOMERS OUT OF THE BOX

WHAT ABOUT US, NOW?

> *"Love is a game that two can play and both win."*
> Eva Gabor

Even though dating has evolved significantly across generations, and seniors have more options than ever before, most of us are new to the many opportunities to connect. Some of us haven't dated in decades and are intimidated by our lack of experience. It can be like starting all over, as in high school, with butterflies, insecurity, and feelings of vulnerability. So, what can we do? Where do we begin?

> We can't expect to find Prince (or Princess) Charming by merely waiting for the phone or doorbell to ring - just like we aren't going to win the lottery if we don't buy a ticket.

Becoming Active

If one is in a retirement home of sorts and newly single, it is quite possible that a person of interest with a pie or a bouquet of flowers may knock on the door; but for those who live in the "real" world, don't count on it. We can, and must, take an active role and reach out. This could include joining more groups or meetups dedicated to hobbies, sports, religion, causes, volunteering, social clubs, etc. Activities we actually enjoy will be easier to follow through on and more successful in finding matches with whom we have something in common. Joining a motorcycle club to meet men makes little sense if one doesn't care about motorcycles. The subject will become boring and unsustainable. That is not to say that we need to have identical interests, but it's better to begin by seeking others with whom we have some things in common. Another consideration for us to remember is that hanging out in stripper bars or joining quilting circles are valid activities for making friends but not conducive to forming successful relationships with members of the opposite sex.

CHAPTER 5: MODERN DATING

As a pilot beginning in 1964, I have seen the growth in participation of women interested in flying careers. Few people continue flying into their seventies, so I wondered where I might find former female pilots to date. I thought that maybe they had settled into radio-controlled model airplane and drone clubs, so I checked some out. Not a woman to be seen in any of them. Back to eharmony!

Remembering to keep an open mind, our prospective partner's involvement in an activity that we have never been interested in, say ballet, gives us an opportunity to learn and reconsider our prejudice. As an example, for those who have never been interested in ballet, watching the all-nude ballet in the film *Clockwork Orange* may lead some to a new appreciation of the art. Just saying.

Our Own Backyards

You could start in your own backyard, simply by listing all the singles (of the preferred gender) you know who have any possibility of being a match. You can include people you used to know from work, religious activities, or other groups. An open mind and a new perspective could be applied to people you had never thought of in this new context.

Next, you can solicit suggestions from your family and good friends. The thought of a blind date might bring a mixture of fear, boredom, and nausea to many, but a friend of a friend might not be the stereotypical cinematic disaster. There is credibility in linked friendships that are known quantities that will typically protect you from wackos and serial killers. Speaking of blind dates, if your friends really want to set up a party or whatever for you, it might be better for everyone that it be an activity with sufficient people so that you can be relaxed and casual. In that way, you don't feel you are the focus of everyone's attention.

Speed Dating

Speed dating can be an effective way to meet prospective matches. As some have lost faith in the efficacy of online dating, interest in speed dating has resurged in various regions. These in-person events are organized and run by a range of sponsors, and the procedures and rules vary greatly. Most will advertise aiming at specific ages and applicable gender preferences. Typical group size for heterosexuals is around a dozen each of men and women.

Participants may sit face-to-face for a short period – typically 1 to 5 minutes – while they share a bit of information about themselves. When the timer goes off or the whistle blows, they move on to the next dater. After everyone has met, participants submit a list of whom they would like to see again. The organizer examines the lists to determine which individuals have mutual attraction. Each are then notified later of their matches and given the requisite contact information. Fraternization at events, other than during the X-minute date period, is often not encouraged, and may be prohibited. Exchange of contact data during the date period can be frowned upon or prohibited. The rules are typically strict to offer a bit of security and to save the embarrassment of face-to-face rejections.

Variations of the theme are also popular with more casual interactions feeling more like a mixer party. Add-on activities, like DJ's and dancing, allow additional socialization.

When searching online for local speed dating events, it may be difficult to sort out true, in person speed dating events from smaller, regular, elite, or specialized online dating sites, and other custom services that have hijacked the term. If you want to experience face-to-face speed dating, persistence is necessary.

Power Up the Internet

Online dating is an extremely powerful tool for meeting potential matches. It's popularity in all adult age brackets is high, despite its flaws and problems. The websites vary significantly in terms of targeted audiences, matching algorithms, rules, tools, services, cost, and ease of use. The business models are different for hookup sites, like Tinder, than for long-term apps or websites (Match, eharmony....). Most of the senior oriented sites are of the latter form. The participants are typically matched by age, location, interests, personality, education, etc. A possible downside is that there

CHAPTER 5: MODERN DATING

can be a great deal of time required to enter the information needed to feed the analysis software in sites like eharmony, and many participants aren't willing to put much effort into completing the process.

Additionally, since the goal of all businesses includes making money, when a long-term match is made, the company loses two customers. As a result, some of the online companies are beginning to enhance their business models and augment their programs to include in-person events.

All online sites have security issues with scammers, some of whom can be hard to detect. Roughly a third of online users believe they have been catfished: matched with false profiles by nefarious groups using various tricks. The scammer encourages unwitting users to divulge personal information or eventually send money. Seniors are lucrative targets.

Another problem is that some daters create misleading profiles through undated younger pictures, understated ages, and false resumes. In general, slightly bogus profiles may be merely hooks for the insecure to get a date. The person may fear that presenting the truth will not garner interest, so they create something that might, with the hope that "When they meet the real me, I can wow them."

Despite the negatives we just discussed, recent overall data show that:

- 19% of internet users are online daters, and 20% of those are seniors over 65.
- Roughly 75% of all online daters are seeking long-term relationships.
- Most importantly, the majority of users claim the same or more successful experiences online than from other sources of meeting in person.
- The online dating growth rate is robust at over 10% per year.

My personal experience in the San Francisco Bay area has been excellent. I have been dating online for five years on and off. The women that I have met have all been intelligent, lovely, and very enjoyable to be with. I've made some great friends and have recently found the one I have every reason to believe is The One.

Getting Ready

There has been a significant amount of research to measure both quantity and quality of various aspects of online dating. Pew Research Center published "10 Facts About Online Dating in 2019" [5.3]. These data reflect all ages:

- Women are more likely to care about a prospect's profile information than men are.

- Just how much information you include on your dating profile can influence how many matches you get. According to the Pew Research Center, if you're seeking to match with a woman, more is better.

- About 72% of women think it's essential to list the type of relationship you're looking for, (long-term, friendship, etc.) compared to 53% of men.

- When it comes to personal information, 32% of women and 18% of men want to know about a match's religious beliefs, and 27% of women and 8% of men are curious about the other person's occupation. Height seems to be a factor as well: 22% of women but only 8% of men want to know how tall a potential match is.

- Political affiliation appears to be relatively unimportant at just 18% for women and 10% for men.

CHAPTER 5: MODERN DATING

Figure 9. Getting support from our kids and grandkids for online dating.

BOOMERS OUT OF THE BOX

CHAPTER 6: ONLINE DATING PROCESS

"Anything worth doing good takes a little chaos"

Flea

In the beginning, online dating may seem overwhelming; maybe even a little chaotic. It's a lot like trying to take a drink of water out of a firehose. The offerings appear incredible, the variety immense, and the presentations seem much like toaster listings on Amazon.

Some approach online dating with enthusiasm and high expectations. Others view dating in general, with reluctance and skepticism. With an open mind, relaxed attitude, and a desire to have fun along the way, online dating can become an enjoyable adventure that ultimately results in an enduring relationship.

Before you begin making your plans, creating your profile, and actually meeting people, it may be useful to gain some perspective on the whole online dating process. Let's examine the phases that you are likely to encounter as you navigate this unique dating environment.

PHASE 1: THE CANDY STORE

A note of caution: if it looks too good to be true....

Once you have your profile in place, photos of suggested matches from the service provider will begin appearing. At this point, it's typically hard not to get excited and start creating a list of attractive potential matches to research further. And every day, new candy is delivered to your inbox, and the process continues anew.

Since perceived attractiveness is the first attribute of the potential matches that is presented to you, my suggestion is to retain a broader group until you have reviewed the text or narrative parts of their profiles and make decisions based upon more information.

Typically, the person who is presented by the provider is not aware that his or her profile has been sent to you, nor is this person necessarily seeing you appear as a match for him or her. *Premium* subscriptions on many packages, however, will notify you when you are viewed.

You can click on "Like" (or some other icon depending on the service provider) to indicate that you would like to begin a dialogue with a particular person. Some participants will ignore "likes" if they do not include a personalized message.

Responses to your messages or "likes" can be immediate, especially on hookup sites, but often they can take time. Some people check their messages regularly once or twice a day, others may not check back for several days or even weeks. When a person is otherwise occupied (with dating, traveling, health issues, etc.), it can sometimes take longer. You can also expect that people are communicating with multiple prospects at any given time.

CHAPTER 6: ONLINE DATING PROCESS

PHASE 2: ELECTRONIC CONTACT

Our first interactions may lead to dialogues with the "worthy" matches. Initially, communication is exclusively via the site messaging system since no other contact information is provided. Exchanging short messages to ask and answer questions can expand into more lengthy conversations.

> **Tip:** While this message format is adequate for getting started, the website word processors are not particularly user friendly when trying to write multiple paragraphs. However, you can compose your prose on your own word processor and copy/paste it into the website or app. Note that some services (such as Match) won't allow pasting on the first message, so one can say "Hi Pat" as the first message, then follow up immediately with a pasted message.

If both parties pass this first hurdle, they may advance to the text, phone, or email stage. It is suggested that for security the next step be email, and that you create this email account specifically for dating. This is especially important if your email address identifies you, such as jane.doe36@gmail.com. A new generic address, such as dater123@gmail.com, can be created. A burner phone account could be used to add another level of security for texting or calling, even though most phones have contact blocking features.

Depending on the individuals, this phase can end quickly with rejection by either party or can continue for a couple of days to weeks or even months, until the next step, which is to meet in person.

> *Note: Some participants believe it is better to get to the face-to-face phase as soon as possible. This is to ensure that the prospect is real and not a bot or scammer from Nigeria.*

PHASE 3: THE FIRST DATE IS A MEET-AND-GREET

This initial meet-and-greet serves the purpose of establishing the credibility of a match and the possibility of moving forward into formal dating. First impressions, followed by demeanor, personality, physical appearance, and a host of character traits are on display for both people to observe. When participation at the first meeting is split equally between the parties, it allows both people to give and receive information and insight. The next chapter delves into the first date in detail and provides guidance, some of which will be applicable to meet-and-greets as well as subsequent dates.

As noted earlier, a common complaint about these first meetings is that many people are turned off when the meeting feels like a business interview. "*A rose by any other name is still a rose.*" However, this meeting doesn't have to feel like an impersonal interview; it's a conversation, not an interrogation. Often, if you converse as you would with any new person, inquiring into their interests and family, you will have an enjoyable time and learn some things. Even if the person isn't The One, maybe he or she could become a friend.

If you should decide you'd like to take it further and see each other again, remember that it is common at this point for both people to be also vetting (dating) others simultaneously. It should not be expected that after some phone conversations and a first date that anyone would be so certain that they would instantly become exclusive. It took several months for the Golden Bachelor to whittle down 25 to one, and we know how that turned out.

CHAPTER 6: ONLINE DATING PROCESS

PHASE 4: REAL DATING

The dating process allows time for us to really get to know one another. Thinking back to our younger years, it usually took weeks or months before we advanced to the stage of "going steady". And even then, the steady relationship often dissolved quickly. But now, until a couple decides they want to be exclusive, it is to be expected that both parties are still dating others. This is not a bad thing. As seniors, time passes quickly, and many are watching the clock while feeling a bit of urgency. It is natural that we want to get things wrapped up as soon as possible, while at the same time, we want to be confident that we are making the right choices.

Dating multiple people can be difficult to manage, but it does save time and takes advantage of the then-current website dating pool. During this phase, romance and sex may or may not be on the table, but it is important that both parties communicate that their relationship is neither committed nor exclusive so there are no misunderstandings.

> **Non-Monogamous Relationships:** Non-monogamous consensual relationships are on the rise with seniors according to multiple sources. It is important that those with the intent to enter such relationships discuss this with their matches early on to avoid wasted time and shattered expectations. These discussions are often awkward because some don't expect others to be dating multiple matches at the same time.
>
> As we age, long-distance relationships, separate living arrangements, and the desire for greater time apart may favor having multiple partners. Retirement communities sometimes popularize a hookup mentality that fosters more open types of relationships. You may want to keep an open mind and examine the possibilities.

PHASE 5: EXCLUSIVE DATING

This is the final phase in the dating process. This period of dating is intended to explore compatibility and chemistry. Sufficient time together will hopefully lead to the array of experiences required to determine the degree to which your wants and needs are met. Additionally, questions and concerns can be addressed by both parties. No matches are likely to align perfectly, but through honest and open conversations and objective evaluation, you can decide whether or not you want to carry the relationship further.

CHAPTER 6: ONLINE DATING PROCESS

MY STORY – OF COURSE IT IS UNIQUE

Thinking that my personal experiences with online dating might prove to be useful for those of you just starting out, I offer the following:

In 2019, was living in Vieques, Puerto Rico when my partner died. I was devastated and wanted to establish a new relationship quickly. The dating pool in my location was slim to none, so I decided to attempt to find a new partner in the San Francisco Bay Area, where my sons lived. I briefly researched dating apps and selected eharmony because it reviewed well with seniors.

> *My thoughts at the time were that I might find someone who would like to spend some time in the Caribbean with me, and I would spend some time in the Bay Area with her. I was hoping for a third together in Vieques, another third together in California, and the last third apart at our respective homes. It looked good on paper - to me.*

So, I answered the myriad questions on eharmony, and I listed my son's address, but I explained in the narrative that I was living in Puerto Rico, etc. How did that work? Well enough to message back and forth with nearly a dozen promising prospects. Near the end of 2019, I traveled to the Bay Area for two weeks to meet four women that I had identified as good potential matches. They turned out to be wonderful women, but I felt the chemistry was really great with one over the others.

I returned several weeks later, and Annie (my match) and I decided to give the relationship a go. She came down to Vieques and had a wonderful time. I came to visit her in March of 2020 for a couple weeks just as the pandemic broke out, and we hunkered down together until November. We had a great time, but primarily due to one of us being quite emotionally sensitive and the other not having much emotional intelligence (low EQ), we started falling apart in September.

BOOMERS OUT OF THE BOX

Shortly thereafter, it was over, and I was left dazed and confused.

This was the first time in my life that a person I loved broke off our relationship, and I didn't understand how it could have happened. I was a veteran of a 39-year marriage and a 12-year partnership; surely, I knew what I was doing; or were the previous women in my life exceptions to the norm and merely easy to get along with? I did a lot of soul searching and began studying this emotional intelligence thing. It took me almost a year before I felt confident and ready to re-enter the dating space. So, I signed up for eharmony again and repeated the process.

> In the Bay Area there are many high-quality women on the dating sites, so from the beginning, I attempted to maintain contact with a large number of potential matches. I initially used a spreadsheet to log communications and track results for each woman. This made it possible to keep matches straight and to test the effectiveness of different early message "hooks" that would get responses. (Yes, I am a Geek at times, but I can hide it for a while. **After we pass the chemistry test, the tech side of me unsurprisingly becomes viewed as an asset by senior women.**)

After many messages, texts, and phone conversations, I again culled my list, returned to the Bay Area (January 2023), and met another five women – all interesting, intelligent, and fun to be with. Again, one stood out, and we seemed to have the chemistry. Barbara and I dated for a couple months or so, and it all appeared to be going quite well, but out of nowhere she broke it off. No triggering event, no argument, no harsh words, just "pickup your stuff". I was stunned, but I had started to realize that this might be the new normal, and that I had better get used to it.

> Part of dating is a numbers game. We've seen the Dating Game and the Bachelor TV shows with the premise that we can find a perfect match from three or twenty-five candidates, but that's rarely true. Although most of us know these TV shows are not real life, they

CHAPTER 6: ONLINE DATING PROCESS

can color our expectations. We may need to remind ourselves that "none of the above" is the appropriate answer where our task is to select one person from whatever group we are presented with. We need to understand that we are searching for one among the potentially unlimited number of matches we will be given, and it can take time for the right one to come along.

I jumped back into search mode, and by August or so, I found another wonderful woman, Charlotte, and we began the dance of love. She was in California during the fall and summer and lived near her daughter and grandkids. She spent much of the winter and spring in New Orleans, at her primary residence. She, too, visited Vieques, and I visited her in Louisiana. That fall, I realized that it was time for me to relocate back to the Bay Area full-time and completed the move in February.

Note: My concept of living apart part-time may work for some, but it was NOT appealing to any of the many women with whom I corresponded. Although my goal was to continue living part of my life on the waterfront of a tropical island and the other part in beautiful California, it was not consistent with my desire to establish a primary romantic mate. Discovering this reality, I was hugely disappointed, but once I recognized what was most important to me, I moved back to California to pursue my love life.

Shortly thereafter, she sent me a beautiful love letter from New Orleans ending our relationship because she thought with her travel, the time apart wasn't going to work. I was severely disappointed, but I was becoming accustomed to rejection. Nonetheless, we had shared a great time together and have remained friends. I quickly moved on.

I started writing this book in earnest immediately after arriving in the Bay Area. As part of my research, I investigated other online dating sites and decided to add Match.com due to its popularity in the Bay Area, and it gave me many more potential matches to contact. I again began meeting and dating a number of charming and accomplished women.

BOOMERS OUT OF THE BOX

Several months later, Charlotte returned for the summer, and she said that she wanted to get together again. I was seriously dating others but, given that I was still very fond of her, I asked if a close friends with benefits relationship would be alright because I intended to continue dating. She agreed.

> My research had taken me on a tour of many relationship types, and in the spirit of open mindedness, I had come out of my serial monogamous mode to consider some of the other options. I thought if I tried them, maybe I'll like them.

That lasted until the end of August when Charlotte decided she needed an exclusive relationship. Although I was involved with a half dozen other matches, I realized that I would rather dedicate myself to her than lose her completely. I called each of the women I was dating to cancel the scheduled dates. I asked if they would still like to go out as friends, and only Diane (whom I'd yet to meet in person) said yes.

Diane and I met for the first time for lunch. She was a very accomplished author and was interested in this book I was writing. I was very impressed with her, and we met for another lunch to discuss more about the book.

I had mentioned to Charlotte that, despite my extreme modesty, I felt the need to check out a local nudist or naturist camp. I wanted to experience what it felt like to be naked in front of others, find out why people wanted to be in a group in the buff, and how all of this might relate to body positivity. I asked her if she wanted to come with me, and while she said she would, it was clear she would rather not. I mentioned this to Diane as we were talking about the book, and she said she was game if Charllotte didn't want to go, so I let Charlotte off the hook.

I picked up Diane, and off we went on a perfectly beautiful day for the great adventure. It turns out that the parking lot was the locker room. Our naked guide arrived at the car and said that as soon as we stripped down to the bare essentials (shoes), he would show us around. Without hesitation or embarrassment, off came our clothes as we were both overcome with a feeling of unexpected liberation. We spent

CHAPTER 6: ONLINE DATING PROCESS

most of the day in or around the pool, but also took a nature hike, played a little 8-ball pool, and shared a potluck dinner with our fellow nudists.

> *An interesting phenomenon becomes obvious when you spend a day conversing with someone totally nude. You tend to surrender your natural defenses. When you intentionally bare all, you are at the height of vulnerability. You can comfortably talk about almost anything. Diane and I shared thoughts and stories we had never spoken about with anyone else, and we barely (no pun intended) knew each other.* [4]

We had such a deep intellectual and emotional connection (nothing romantic) that we decided to date. I asked Charlotte if we could go back to the good FWB relationship, but she was not up for it. I lobbied for a couple of weeks to no avail. With a great sense of loss, we ended our existing relationship. The new relationship with Diane blossomed, and I am now confident that she is The One.

At one point in my journey to enlightenment, I thought that I could be quite happy in simultaneous romantic relationships with both Charlotte and Diane. In retrospect, I was wrong. Despite my strong feelings for Charlotte, I could only manage to focus on one person, and that person turned out to be Diane. This is apparently my truth.

> *Final note: As one can see, I have experienced many ups and downs in my series of relationships. I have had many more dating failures than successes. But the one constant throughout this journey is that **I have enjoyed the process**. I have had a great deal of fun, met wonderful people, and learned a lot. And, of course, I found The One.*
>
> *I have learned that it is important to bounce back quickly from rejection. Even though on some level it is personal, my advice is to just not take it personally*

---

[4] My recommendation if you decide to try this yourself is to go with a friend or friends on a busy day so that there are many folks to meet and talk with. It's a great ice breaker for a new prospect.

BOOMERS OUT OF THE BOX

because it wouldn't have been a good fit if you both weren't equally smitten. Besides, there is nothing you can do about it. If you keep at it, one day you may silently thank them for freeing you to find The One.

CHAPTER 6: ONLINE DATING PROCESS

BOOMERS OUT OF THE BOX

CHAPTER 7: WHO ARE WE NOW?

"Know thy self"

Socrates

ARE WE READY FOR A NEW COMMITMENT OR RELATIONSHIP?

Roughly 39 million seniors in the U.S. are single. Many of us are lonely[5] and miss companionship and intimacy. If you are one of them, you are likely seeking a new relationship of some kind.

As single seniors, it is important for us to realize that we have entered a new phase of our lives and now is a perfect time to consider a reset or reboot that includes entering a new relationship. Most of us are retired, lost our spouses (through death or divorce), are not as physically fit as we used to be, and are not very facile with dating online or otherwise. But we're thinking we may be ready.

What does "being ready for a relationship" really mean? It means being emotionally available and includes having our legal, physical, and mental houses in order. All of us have baggage, an accumulation of active issues and experiences

---

[5] Data from a 2024 Pew study and reported by The Senior List [7.4] states that:

In 2023, over a third of adults between the ages of 50 and 80 report feeling socially isolated in the preceding year. 37 percent of older adults report that they feel a lack of companionship....

The report also indicated that less favorable health factors contributed to greater levels of loneliness:

Nearly three-quarters (73 percent) of those who reported fair to poor mental health report feeling a lack of companionship (compared to 33 percent of those reporting good mental health).

stored in our heads, hearts, and self-storage units. This is totally normal and not necessarily a problem; but it can be.

We need to have a clear picture of who we are and review our current situations. Some conditions are obvious, and some may be unfixable. The following includes some areas to consider:

Legal & Financial

In-depth discussion on individual situations is beyond the scope of this book, but you need to check some boxes before reaching out to potential matches. Are you legally single? Are you free of relevant financial encumbrances or potential bankruptcies? Are you involved in lawsuits or court orders (bail, judgements, parole, probation, restraining, etc.) that can have a significant impact? Do you have other personal obligations that might also be obstacles to forming the perfect union? If these are problem areas for you, maybe the timing is not appropriate for establishing a new relationship.

Physical Condition

Are you physically healthy? At some point, sharing the nature of your situations will be required. Do you have mobility limitations? Do you have diseases, conditions, and/or disorders? Are you fit or are you suffering from hearing, visual, or sexual impairments? Are you taking action to correct issues that have known cures or partial solutions such as exercise, hearing aids,[6] glasses, canes, diet, medications, etc.?

Mental & Emotional States

Are you experiencing negative or unstable emotions? Do your moods swing quickly or wildly? Are you overly inclined to argue or find fault with others? Do you often feel hurt by

---

[6] Note that according to a study by Achieve Healthy Aging:

…results, published in the Lancet in 2024, showed that in older adults at increased risk for cognitive decline, hearing intervention slowed down loss of thinking and memory abilities by 48% over 3 years. [7.1]

Apple currently offers self-fitting software for their iPhone ear buds as remarkably good hearing aids for moderate hearing loss.

CHAPTER 7: WHO ARE WE NOW?

friends, families, or acquaintances? Do you frequently find yourself the victim of others' actions? Are you addicted to gambling, alcohol, or other substances?

Are you free of impactful mental conditions? This is a question that may be beneficial to figure out. While you may be quick to realize that you're sick when you have a fever and are vomiting, when you're just feeling off and not yourself, you might not realize that you're suffering from depression, grief, loss, PTSD, or other issues.

Some of our potential mental/emotional conditions can be successfully self-diagnosed and self-treated, possibly with the aid of self-help books. But professional help in the form of therapy, treatments, and/or medications may be required to cure or treat many of the potential conditions mentioned above.

Other Issues

Most of us have one or more other sources of stress that may include a recent divorce, family issues, projects in progress, relocation, work, or other commitments. Is this good timing? Do you have too much going on to be able to commit the time and effort required to work on relationship building? Do you feel undue pressure to get into a relationship quickly? Have you put the cart before the horse?

Once you have settled on who you are, you can decide if you wish to remain on the same course, continue your existing lifestyle, maintain your current living arrangements, etc. You also can seek to improve your social skills and personality traits in the context of becoming better suited for relationship building and engaging with a whole new world. Nothing is off the table, and you can reinvent yourself if you so desire.

Approximately 90% of our senior population over 65 have been married. It stands to reason that many single seniors are grieving their loss, whether from death or divorce. In this case, loneliness may become a companion, and depression can set in. We might not recognize our condition initially, but we need to determine whether we are grieving, and if so, what the cause might be. We can't be ready for a new relationship if we are still grieving our loss from the last one.

BOOMERS OUT OF THE BOX

There are many books available to guide us through the process. I, personally, gleaned enough from one such book to get past this obstacle, but the result surprised me.

CHAPTER 7: WHO ARE WE NOW?

BOOMERS OUT OF THE BOX

CHAPTER 8: CREATING A PLAN FOR ACTION

"In preparing for battle I have always found that plans are useless, but planning is indispensable."

Dwight D. Eisenhower

Now that we've identified our own baggage, determined the type of relationship we intend to pursue, and learned a bit about modern dating, how do we proceed? What's the plan for achieving the results we envision? There are generally multiple ways to solve the challenges we face, so it's our task to find the best one we can – the optimal one for each of us. They all start with forming our expectations and adopting an attitude that fosters success.

Regardless of the type of long-term relationship you are seeking, there are significant advantages to thinking of every potential match as a friend first. There is less pressure when you first build a foundation based on getting to know someone before pursuing a higher goal. As you begin to form a friendship, you can also explore other relationship options as you wish.

If you establish a friendship that lacks the chemistry to fulfil your needs, you still have a new friend. If you find that the match is not friendship material at any point, you can end the process with rejection.

BOOMERS OUT OF THE BOX

SETTING OUR EXPECTATIONS

> *"Love has nothing to do with what you are expecting to get - only with what you are expecting to give - which is everything."*
>
> Katharine Hepburn

Why are expectations so critical in creating a satisfying result? A very, very short story may illustrate the point.

Scenario 1:

A plumber gives Smith an estimate of $1,000 to repair a broken sewer line. The final invoice comes out to $1,500.

Scenario 2:

A plumber gives Smith an estimate of $2,000 to repair a broken sewer line. The final invoice comes out to $1,500.

Conclusion:

In both cases the cost came out to be the same, but in Scenario 1, Smith was not happy because he expected a lower cost and didn't get it, while in Scenario 2, Smith's expected cost was significantly higher, but his actual cost came out lower, which made him very happy. Meeting or exceeding expectations is a big plus, while not meeting them is always a disappointment.

Developing realistic expectations in the many steps of the dating process can be daunting, especially if you are an online dating newbie. Lowering expectations is not the same as lowering standards; it is merely an attempt to become more realistic and to avoid disappointment.

What we can expect:

- Thinking about the dating pool. Over a third of the 65 and over population is single, and two thirds of those singles are women. The statistics further indicate that there are roughly twice as many single women as men

CHAPTER 8: CREATING A PLAN FOR ACTION

in this age group. According to a Pew survey, 16% of the cohort are actively looking for a relationship and that a woman's chance of finding a successful relationship is half that of a man's. This is caused in part because women live longer than men, and historically, men marry younger women.

- In work, school, religious pursuits, hobbies, clubs, and other such activities, participants are not necessarily seeking new relationships. It can be difficult (and potentially cause anxiety) trying to determine who in the group may also be looking for a mate. With online or speed dating, the mere fact one is signed up is usually proof enough. The exception is the case of a "helpful" friend or relative who has signed up somebody and built a profile for them before they were ready.

- How many prospects does it take to find THE ONE? We can't say with any degree of certainty because there are too many variables. We might have friends and family members who can offer qualified matches because they understand us and know individuals who fit – or not. The speed dating provider might prequalify the invited group well – or not. The online app may include software that is effective at scoring matching prospects – or not. We can, however, gain some perspective from our history. Looking back to high school, college, or any occasion when we were in a sexually mixed group with others of the same age for any length of time, did we (or could we) find a match? How big a dating pool is required? 10? 100? 1,000?

- If the goal is to find friends rather than a romantic partner, the requirements may be less restrictive and more flexible, so the qualifying percentage could be higher. Not only that, those focusing only on finding The One are more likely to get frustrated and lose interest.

- There are limitations on the number and quality of the leads (matches) presented, depending upon the service and subscription being used. If the list is composed of random people, it may be a waste of our time. The better the system used for determining matches, the fewer deletes or removes that will be required before finding keepers. The quality of the matches provided is extremely important. Some of the boutique matching services offer personal investigation and selection of matches rather than computer generated results, but they are expensive and also vary significantly in success rates.

- Dating profiles can be scant on some sites. The reasons vary, but online services typically have tiered pricing, and at the "free" level, the amount of detailed information presented may be meager. Some profile generalities one might experience:
    - A portion of the daters are not that into it. Maybe they were frustrated or lonely one night and joined on a whim. Perhaps a friend badgered them into joining. Sometimes friends and family make the profile to "help".
    - Some participants aren't who they pretend to be and use no pictures or information that could identify them because they are married, public figures, or recognizable to fellow workers or other associates.
    - Some are fakes. (See Chapter 12 for more on this subject.)
    - As we age, some of us are reluctant to upload our pictures or write about ourselves due to insecurities or embarrassment.
    - Between 75% & 88% of Boomers use the internet, but many are not facile. Loading, entering data, keeping current with changes, and using many of the online apps can hamper and frustrate the less technical users. This leads to minimal profiles and less engagement by members.

CHAPTER 8: CREATING A PLAN FOR ACTION

- o Laziness, lack of understanding, pessimism, or other inhibitions can further reduce the quality and usefulness of some profiles.

- o Boomers without recent dating experience can be very guarded or clueless regarding how to act or proceed, leading them to inadvertently send mixed or confusing signals.

- Advancing from the online service to email, text, phone calls, facetime, zoom calls, and face-to-face is one typical progression seen in online dating. With some matches, this proceeds at a rapid pace and steps are even skipped. With others, it's a slower process. With some, the pace is intentional, but others are slower, busy, or engaged with multiple matches. Generally, men are not into writing emails or texting for an extended period. Women, on the other hand, may want to play it safer and get to feel more confident about the match before giving out personal information and meeting in-person. Or, in some cases, daters want to meet as soon as possible to ensure the match is real. Keep in mind that relationships can only move as fast as the slower participant.

- The horror stories we hear about that initial in-person meeting are sometimes true: the profile picture that is 20 years old and not dated, the age that is underreported by a decade, or the personality that is quite different from what the correspondence implied. All of these can happen, but most are pretty straightforward and honest. The good news is when we receive a pleasant surprise with details that weren't obvious from the profile.

- On the overly optimistic side, both parties may feel that they've found the perfect match after just a few dates, and while it may be true love, it may also merely be delightful infatuation. More time may be needed. Our strong desire to meet The One and start a new life together before we get too old could blind us to our irrational exuberance and lead us into a doomed relationship.[7] But it is often possible to have a lasting love at first sight.[8]

- Rejection can come at any time in the process. First, many rejections happen without our knowledge. We don't know when our profile is presented to someone unless they choose to view or pursue us. Second, if we submit a "Like" of a new profile and hear nothing back, we aren't necessarily sure whether we were deleted or just put on the shelf for later. Next it can happen after a brief or extended correspondence, or even after meeting in-person. We can't take this personally. It's not necessarily about us. It could be politics, hair color, demographics, or a myriad of other details. So, maybe we don't ski, and the match is looking for a ski partner. It can, and often is, a lack of romantic chemistry. Chemistry is neither logical nor controllable; it is not subject to reason or discretion. We can't change it by intent or effort. Most of us know and like hundreds of people, but with how many do we share romance? Probably none. It's not personal.

> *"You can never control who you fall in love with, even when you're in the most sad, confused time of your life. You don't fall in love with people because they're fun. It just happens."*
>
> Kirsten Dunst

- We can't expect a successful long-term relationship to be determined through a few weeks or months of dating

---

[7] This has happened twice to me personally. Nonetheless, they were wonderful people and are treasured friends. I'm very happy to know them and have zero regrets.

[8] There is also some evidence that love can render people oblivious to a new partner's faults — the "love is blind" phenomenon. Lucy Brown, a professor of neuroscience at Albert Einstein College of Medicine, found that when some study participants were shown pictures of their lover early in a relationship, they had less activity in a part of the prefrontal cortex, the area important for decision-making and evaluating others. The findings suggest that we might "suspend negative judgments of the person we're in love with," she said. [8.1]

CHAPTER 8: CREATING A PLAN FOR ACTION

because we are initially in a zone of infatuation, hope, expectation, and excitement. *"The truth is that we love to be in love....Since at the outset we actually know very little about the real person, we can't truly love them in any meaningful sense of the word. When we fall "head over heels" for someone, we are usually aware only of relatively superficial elements about them, characteristics that have powerfully impressed us during the short time we've spent together. We are easily inclined to make more of these than they ultimately may be worth, and it is quite common to be surprised and even shocked when we discover later what we assumed about the person turned out not to be true at all. Alas, some people never seem to stop falling in love with love...."* [8.2] It's nearly impossible to see the many sides of a person when we are eager and hurried. We've probably all known people who could mask, hide, or control their less pleasant aspects for long periods of time and then blow up, act out, or display a darker side. As in any form of partnership, we don't initially see the responses and behaviors caused by stress and conflict. It takes time for these situations to potentially emerge. Even the chronicled marriage of the first Golden Bachelor ended in divorce after only 3 months due to irreconcilable differences that might have been discovered during courtship if more time had been spent dating.

- We need not fret or regret failed attempts at a long-term relationship. If we are having a good time getting to know someone, that can be a huge positive, whether or not it lasts. Maybe a meaningful friendship can evolve. While the end of a romance can be a major disappointment, hopefully we can learn more about ourselves and about interpersonal relationships. When we get back on the horse, we will be better prepared for The Next One.

BOOMERS OUT OF THE BOX

Reflections from Barbara

An Experienced Online Dater on a Breakup:

> *I don't believe that inauthenticity was the issue. We just weren't together long enough to truly know one another. I think that in many cases, we are initially attracted to someone, and in a short time, we build images of the whole person from very little data, through extrapolation. Our expectations are formed in part by our own hopes and wishes. When we were younger, it was a process similar to infatuation followed by loss of interest as we got to know someone better. As seniors, we probably don't want to date for 3 or more years before making some kind of a commitment to a partner.*
>
> *In my case, there were some pink flags, but I don't give up easily if I believe there is hope. I don't fault myself or the man I was with. I attribute the breakup to the reality that we just weren't sufficiently compatible, and that's the question we're trying to answer through dating -* **the system worked**.

It's critical that our expectations are realistic to avoid disappointment and frustration. It is understandable that many of us will need to lower our expectations. However, some may feel that they have to lower their expectations so much that they no longer feel dating is worth the effort, and that's not good.

CHAPTER 8: CREATING A PLAN FOR ACTION

IMPLEMENTING THE PLAN

"A goal without a plan is a wish."

Jeff Rich

So far in this chapter, we've set our expectations and examined how to present ourselves. It's time to combine what we know into an executable plan to reach out and find some prospective matches.

Any plan we create is a working document – nothing is yet cast in stone. Our efforts are experiments that will typically not work as imagined. In order to measure the success of different approaches, we can implement multiple strategies – either simultaneously or sequentially – and use the feedback or results to revise the original plan.

Getting Started Online

The first step requires some upfront logistical decisions. We have the simple task of deciding what computer **and/or** phone we intend to use. Functionality (screen size), convenience (portability), and personal preferences vary. Some sites don't have apps and use only standard webpages that are accessed with standard browsers.

Next, another simple decision for most of us is whether to utilize a full-service online matchmaking service or use the popular and well-known dating websites. Matchmaker sites like Tawkify.com provide personal service, privacy, vetting, and security for high-profile individuals and others who are willing to pay from $5,000 to whatever. The company does the work, but their inventory is limited. To the general public, it appears to operate a bit like a brokerage or talent agency.

Most of us will opt for one of the popular dating sites, but which one? Although we can subscribe to several, we might want to select just one online service initially to keep it simple. Use of online reviews[9] of the various sites, or Googling "best

---

[9] Links to various reviewing sites:
https://money.com/best-senior-dating-websites/

online dating services for seniors", can be somewhat helpful, but almost all reviewing sites acknowledge that they receive compensation from the companies for placement in their rankings. The practice is closer to advertisement than journalism, but they often offer tips and advice on safe dating that are useful.[10]

Location is also a determining variable. Users flock to where other users are, so you'll want to find out which are popular in your area. Small rural communities will typically have a shallow dating pool, and daters often settle on just one or two sites. So, you'll want to check out social media, friends, and online daters who may provide the best guidance for locally popular online dating services. Note that over time, as services change their software or pricing policies, users are likely to migrate to greener pastures.

The price and functionality of the website services are both very important. Each site is unique, and despite its popularity, we need to review their details and/or tutorials – some people will find a site that works great for them, while others may get frustrated with that same site. This is a personal affair. But the most critical criteria in my view are the depth and quality of the dating pool.

Even if a site has a smaller dating pool, if it caters to a narrow group, but one you are interested in, it may bring you greater success than a large pool of the general population. If you want to focus on religion, country, gender, etc., add that to the search. Christianmingle.com caters to Christians and jdate.com to Jewish singles.

Notwithstanding quality ratings, the two most popular sites garnered 78% of the Boomers:

---

https://www.consumeraffairs.com/dating_services/
https://www.cbsnews.com/boston/essentials/hinge-dating-app-review/?intcid=CNM-00-10abd1h
https://www.ncoa.org/adviser/relationships/best-senior-dating-sites/
https://www.forbes.com/search/?q=best+online+dating+sites+for+seniors

[10] MINDBODYGREEN, LLC. [8.3], a women's health-oriented website, is another good source of guidance.

CHAPTER 8: CREATING A PLAN FOR ACTION

- Match.com - 44% of 65 and over
- eharmony.com - 34% of 65 and over

These two popular sites use two very different approaches to matching. Match offers users an opportunity to write a lengthy narrative and answer a few questions to identify their personalities, wants, and needs in a match. Eharmony allows a short narrative and a great number of questions to determine a more thorough personality profile which it uses for grading the matches.[11]

Sites these days generally have multiple levels of subscriptions from free to premium. I'd suggest subscribing monthly during the evaluation to confirm that a particular site meets your needs before committing for a longer period. Monthly subscriptions rates fluctuate over time. Eharmony.com and Match.com are in the $50/month range, while annual agreements are about $25/month. Less popular sites may be half the costs of the popular ones. The free versions of many sites are severely inferior to (**read useless**) the paid versions and may create a negative image of an otherwise acceptable site.

> *Note: Sometimes it's possible to visit the free site a few times and then wait a bit. Reduced cost options may be offered as introductory pricing to hook you and keep you from going elsewhere.*

Many of the sites – even the popular ones – are NOT intuitive and lack road maps and initial setup instructions. Some start off by asking us questions, while not giving us any clue as to where we are going. Some of the services allow us to load, create, and tweak our profiles without going public until we are ready. It can be unwise to launch an incomplete profile in the event your potentially perfect match sees it, isn't impressed, and is never to be seen or heard from again. Some programs send only one member of a proposed match the profile of the other. In that way, if the receiver of the system generated

---

[11] I used both eharmony and match simultaneously to compare them and was matched with several of the same women on both platforms, despite different algorithms. In each case, the match was appropriate.

match isn't interested, the other is neither aware that they were suggested by the service nor that they were rejected.

Joining more than one dating site can become an overwhelming time burden, especially at first. After a month or so, if you are not receiving many qualifying match suggestions, it may be time to recalibrate and consider an additional (or replacement) dating site as well as rewriting your profile and uploading new photos.

Will AI Be Able to Help?

Though in its infancy, Artificial Intelligence is already present in the online dating scene. Some daters are using it to create narratives for profiles as they would any writing task. More incredibly, there are applications that can assume our personas and create messages and maintain a dialogue with prospects or the prospects' AI partners – like two chatbots!

Before we get worried that we are falling hopelessly behind in this technology, note that these apps aren't free, and their effectiveness is not great – yet. How much faith can we have that two chatbots are going to accurately depict their clients' wants, needs, passions, and chemistry? *(I envision two bots "falling in love" and disappearing into the virtual world.)* On the other hand, they may already be useful in separating the wheat from the chaff. Some AI offerings can analyze and critique our dialogues with various matches. Some can act as consultants and suggest questions to ask and responses to match questions. It's an arena that will be filled with AI at some point and worth keeping an eye on.

CHAPTER 8: CREATING A PLAN FOR ACTION

BOOMERS OUT OF THE BOX

CHAPTER 9: THE PROFILE

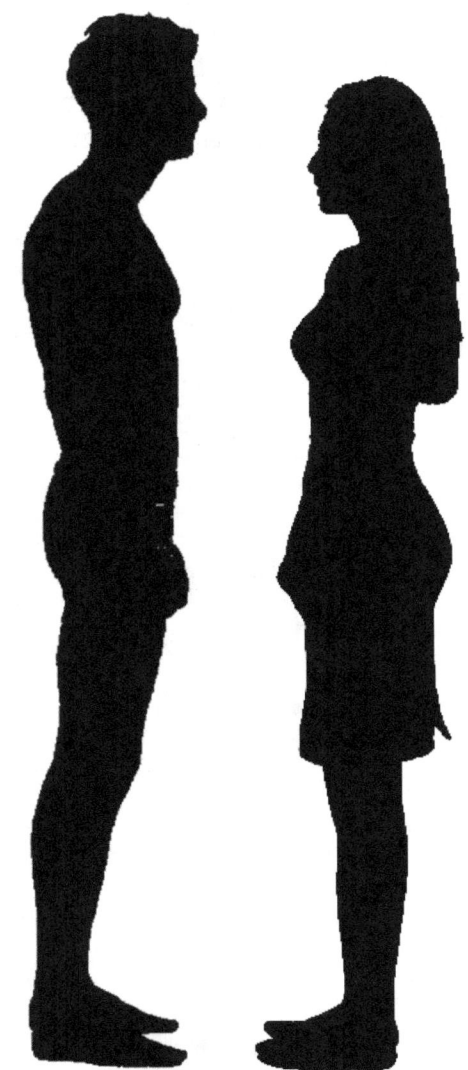

Figure 10. Profiles.

In Chapter 5, we examined preferences for the kind of person you were looking for, The One. Now it's time to put out to the

BOOMERS OUT OF THE BOX

universe who you are in the same way you articulated what you

wanted. The qualities that you list to define yourself, your wishes, and your intentions are helpful in "marketing" yourself to others at any time, whether online, in person in everyday living, or on a date. The purpose of the profile is - like a resume - to **get an interview**. It presents the essentials that can be used when speaking with any potential date.

CHAPTER 9: THE PROFILE

CONSIDERATIONS FOR THE PROFILE

The written profile is a collection of information intended to communicate to the dating world who we are, who we are looking to meet, and what kind of relationship we wish to have. We will also identify and examine issues that you may wish to consider as you create your online profile.

Relationship(s)

Communication from the start should indicate the type of relationship that you are seeking. A brief statement such as: "I am looking forward to establishing a friendship that can lead to a long-term romantic partnership" is clear and complete.

Time & Distance

In Chapter 5 we discussed the necessity of determining how much time you could devote to a relationship, what limits there may be on any commute (related to the distance of homes apart), and whether cohabitation was desired. These are important considerations that you may wish to briefly include in your profile because they could be deal breakers. These issues will come up at some point, so sooner may be better than later.

> *The publicly stated cause of the divorce for the Golden Bachelor was that both parties were close to their families, and the distance became a critical obstacle – Midwest vs. East Coast.*

Personal Traits

Many of us try too hard to cast a wide net and attract everyone. The great majority of our online service provider's suggested matches are not at all suitable matches. So, the process is to separate the wheat from the chaff. Eliminate the chaff so we don't even see those who clearly won't work.

We do want to keep an **open mind**, but if we live and die for wine and ballet, a prospect who lives for fishing and beer, no matter how otherwise attractive, is a real longshot. If they read our profiles, and not just view our pictures, they will delete us and save us from wasting our precious time. So, we must remember to include "deal breakers" in our presentations; however, avoid coming across as a negative person by over-stating things you don't like. As an example, if you love music of certain types but don't care for rock or for large concerts with thousands of people, you could mention that you really love small venues with jazz or chamber music.

Certain assets or attributes are subjective and do not need to be listed in our profiles directly - as either our assets or desired qualities in our matches. Examples include kind, honest, attractive, confident, intelligent, sensitive, and other subjective values. We all know that nobody is looking for someone who is unkind or dishonest. If we state that we have volunteered with a charity for five years, we indirectly communicate who we are more effectively. Properly selected pictures showing us in scenarios we enjoy allow our prospects to determine for themselves whether they may find us attractive.

Preferences

Identifying your likes (and deal-breaking dislikes) helps create a picture of who you are so others can better judge your likely compatibility. Some of the important items on the list could include:

- Drinking, smoking[12], and drug use. Prospective matches may be recovering alcoholics or drug users who don't want to be around other users. Others may shun all use based on religious, health, or philosophical grounds. Time together will disclose if drinking or drugs will adversely affect the behavior of a partner.

- If family activities are a big part of your life, it's important to share that.

- Food constraints can be imposed by allergies, religious beliefs, or personal lifestyle choices like becoming a vegetarian, pescatarian, or vegan. While such limitations may eliminate certain restaurant choices and

---

[12] Smoking prevalence in the United States, lower among seniors 65 and over, is 8.3% compared with younger adults at 22.2%. [9.1].

CHAPTER 9: THE PROFILE

dictate double the meal preparations at home, it is usually manageable. It could be a problem for some people but a perfect match for others.

- Pets and people are not always compatible. Allergies, odors, behaviors (jumping up, barking, humping), defecation, urination, cleanup, etc. are not acceptable to many. Some even become jealous at the time or affection bestowed on pets. On the flipside, others of us are crazy about animals of all kinds.

- Sex is an important subject that needs to be discussed early to ensure that both are on the same page. But in the profile, I suggest that a short mention of your interest is included. For example: "Intimacy and romance are important to me." Additionally, something like this gets the point across: "I'm physically affectionate." If sex is not desired, you might state that, "While I am seeking a very close personal relationship, I am no longer sexually active."

- Socialization is necessary for a healthy life, but how much and what kinds are appropriate for our intended lifestyles? Would any of these statements fit your profile?
    - "I typically entertain in my house or go out with friends at least once a week."
    - "I enjoy more intimate socializing with a couple friends at a time rather than big groups."
    - "I'm not a party person, but I do like doing things with friends."
    - "I prefer to snuggle up in front of a fire most of the time instead of going out."

- Travel for leisure is common among healthy seniors. The options and variations are extensive, from camping to luxury resorts, from forests to museums, from city sights to beaches, and from cruises to sports activities. What's your preference? It's always good to experience new things but be honest about what is more appealing to you. Some may wish to travel often, others not. This needs to be identified in the profile as it is very important to many.

- Other activities we regularly participate in or preferences for things we are looking for in a partner can clearly be added. Examples:
    - "During the season, I go skiing in Breckenridge every weekend, and it would be great if you would join me."
    - "I do yoga every Monday, Wednesday, and Friday morning."
    - "I am in a foursome, and we have a tee-time at 8:15 every Wednesday."

Background, History, &....

It's important to touch enough on your background to explain who you are, where you've been, and what you've been doing. You don't want to boast or bore your potential mates, but you surely want to create interest and offer topics where you might have connections and points in common.

Presentation of your interests & hobbies is useful to add depth to your character and help determine commonalities. Differentiating between former and current activities as well as identifying those in which you participate versus spectate adds additional clarity. You can add and expand on things such as social activities, club participation, and sports.

Our thoughts on the future might be briefly expressed. Again, you want to indicate your intentions going forward, sharing the degree to which you have an **open mind** – that is, are your plans set in concrete or just warm Jell-O?

Religion & Politics

These can be hot button topics. But since the purpose of our profile is to discover like-minded or compatible people, it's a good idea to address these touchy subjects if they are important to you.

CHAPTER 9: THE PROFILE

Religion can be a nonissue for some, especially since procreation is no longer a factor. In many mixed religion relationships "separate but equal" can work. In those situations where religious practices are extensive, it can be more difficult and even undesirable. Religious tolerances vary greatly from person to person.

If you don't care about religion or related practices, you can post it. If you have a loose affiliation, so state. Most importantly, if you have a strong religious connection that might dictate that a match be the same, that filter is a must to cite.

Politics can be addressed in a similar way. Your mission is not evangelism, it's to find matches with whom you're compatible.

Physical Appearance

Some feel that it is shallow or superficial to make an initial judgement based on a photo. Regardless, **few without a posted photo get legitimate serious responses**. Like it or not, for better or worse, when there are many choices available, people will initially filter the options by personal attractiveness. It is impossible to picture ourselves together in a relationship with someone we've never seen. At the end of the day, attractiveness is in the eyes of the beholder, and it varies considerably from person to person.

> *I'm 6'-5' tall, well at least I was. As we age, two things happen: we get shorter, and we deny it. I have met numerous women who claim to be inches taller than they really are. I don't need to look eye to eye with my match, and I am in favor of putting her on pedestal, but not every time I want to kiss her. Therefore, I filter out anyone under 5'-2", figuring they are 5'-0", and that's too much bending over.*

CREATING THE PROFILE

The goal of the profile, the first contact with a potential match, is to advance you forward to the interview process.

> *Your profile should attract just enough attention and interest to elicit a response from a qualifying match.*

Because each dating service is different, it's impossible to provide a universal prototype of the winningest profile. Therefore, we need to set some general guidelines and short examples:

- Brevity. Yes, be as brief as possible while still being clear. The purpose is to provide a broad spectrum of who you are. Save the details for when you actually connect with someone.

- Subjective qualities. Write: "I enjoy volunteering at the food kitchen on Tuesdays and Thursdays" rather than "I'm a generous person."

- Humor. It is hard to "know your audience" when writing your profile. While humor is a positive and desirable attribute, it is often difficult to manage in the profile format. Sarcasm is very often not well received, and complexity can lose the audience. Feedback is pass-fail in the sense that if it is misinterpreted, you may be deleted and not given an opportunity to explain. Nonetheless, if you can pull it off, humor can be a real asset.

- Positive attitude. Upbeat and optimistic profiles are better received. Whininess and complaining are to be avoided. Confidence is valued, but overconfidence may come across as arrogance. Self-deprecating humor is subject to misinterpretation and is best held in reserve until you actually meet in person.

- Independence. It is not uncommon to find potential matches who are in poor health, financially challenged, and are looking for a partner who can support them.

CHAPTER 9: THE PROFILE

Self-sufficiency is highly valued. Including a statement in the profile, such as "I'm in excellent health and financially self-sufficient", can be helpful. Dependency, physical or financial, is a red flag for many potential matches. Honesty is important, and the truth will come out eventually. Women most especially are concerned about the nurse-purse-and-maybe-worse curse.

- Togetherness. Indicate where you are on the continuum of the amount of togetherness you desire with your mate. Togetherness refers to your emotional desire for love, affection, and time together; versus the personal freedom periods you want to pursue work, play, socialization, and family. Most potential matches will want to know your need for alone-time versus face-to-face time. Being too clingy will turn off some, while too much time away will disappoint others. If you are intending to spend a couple of hours a day pursuing fitness (or any other specific activities), it's best to point this out up front.

- Pictures. Photos serve to display many of your physical attributes. Anything difficult to discern, like height and fitness activities can be easily offered in writing. A reasonable approach to marketing is to use a profile image of the best picture of yourself that you can locate, even if it's 10 years old, but DATE STAMP IT. Put the date the picture was taken as part of the title or comment. Likewise, it is essential to have pictures that are current so as not to mislead anyone. Pictures that show you in favorite activities disclose your true self. As a bare minimum, have a current head shot with a great smile and a full body portrait or action shot.
  - For those without high quality current pictures, you can improve your marketing efforts by having a good photographer take your photos. If you have seen some of the selfies and other poor-quality profile images, you will probably agree that you can aim higher.

123

- Photos that look like yearbook or corporate head shots are less enticing when used as the lead image. Other than tuxedos and cocktail dresses, consider using pictures with clothing that is not dominated by black or white; let some colorful items pop out a bit.
- Above all: smile!
- If you are well known or concerned about recognition by colleagues or other specific groups, photos are still important. You can use sunglasses and hats or crop them in a way that hides distinguishing features or your full face. If you are a mayor or congresswoman, lack of anonymity is guaranteed and probably a disqualifier for doing online dating.

- Q&A. Most of the sites have standard questions for you to respond to. You can choose the ones that you feel are relevant.

- Sex. Unless you are looking for a casual sexual relationship, this is not the time to be overly sexy, but a little bit of flirtation can be effective. Those of us who rank sexual attraction at the top of the list might consider posting flirtatious or sexy photos[13] (known as thirst traps) to attract hookups or short-term liaisons. It is not uncommon to pursue both long and short-term relationships simultaneously, but it is probably useful to employ different sites and profiles to keep the two groups separate and not confuse prospects with inconsistent presentations.

- Editing. Make certain grammar and spelling are correct. You can have someone proofread your work. It is probably better to write your content in your trusted word processor and copy the finished work into the online program so that it isn't inadvertently deleted.

---

[13] Sexually explicit photos can get you banned from many of the online sites. Read the terms and conditions for your chosen service.

CHAPTER 9: THE PROFILE

The sites' word processors can't be trusted to behave as one would expect or like.

- Keeping current. As your experiences unfold and your situation changes, you can update your profile to reflect those changes.

Note that everything that you present should be honest and true. In the short term, one can sometimes get away with falsehoods and distortions to attract a mate, but in the long run the truth shall be revealed, trust will be broken, and the relationship will probably be destroyed. It's not worth the effort to pursue a disastrous course. If the truth is not good enough, you've got two valid choices: be honest and see who might still find you among the possibilities, or work on improving yourself to meet a higher standard.

MESSAGING

Messaging is the inevitable and critical next step. It takes the form of a tickler (a "Like" or a "Smile", depending on the site) to initiate a conversation or respond to a suitor's tickler or opening message.

- **The Tickler.** When you find a prospective match whose profile is of interest, reach out with something that will engage them. The tickler will be most effective if it can compliment and respond favorably to something in their profile and ask a related question. Examples include:
    1. "Great picture. I love that area of Yosemite. Have you done the Cook's Meadow Loop lately?"
    2. "I love comedy clubs, too. Have you been to Mac's in Fairfax? They usually have good shows on Wednesday nights. BTW, that's a very cute black dress in the party picture."
    3. "Wow! That's a good-sized bass in the picture. I vacation at Cresent Lake every summer. Where did you catch that one?"
    4. "Great biking photo. Where was that taken?"

Not very useful messages without something personalized include:

    - "Hey! What's up?"
    - "Happy Tuesday!"
    - A "Like" or an emoji without anything specific or personal.

- **The Response.** When receiving a tickler from a prospective match who appears viable, an engaging response is in order. A thanks for a compliment, a return compliment, a response to a question asked, and a question in return provide a format for continuing the interchange. Examples replying to the ticklers above:
    1. "Thanks, I love taking nature photographs. Although it's just a hobby, I have sold quite a few

CHAPTER 9: THE PROFILE

since I retired from architecture. That was my first time to Yosemite; next time I plan to do the Loop. I normally hike in the redwoods north of San Francisco. How about you? I find your history fascinating; you've really led an exciting life."

2. "Thank you, as you might guess, I love to dress up and go dancing. I've not been to Mac's, but I hear it is a fun venue. I normally go to Sweetwater, it's close to home. I read you like to vacation at dude ranches. You look very much at home on a horse, and the hat is perfect. Please tell me more.

3. "Thanks, I won a local contest with that one. I keep my boat at Big Bear Lake about 40 miles north of you. That Cresent area is really nice – I'm envious. I find the picture of you teaching those kids quite attractive. Are they family? I see from your profile that you like to waterski. Are you still doing that? Do you fish at all?"

4. "Thanks, that's from a bike trip around Iceland three years ago. It was a real haul, but Iceland is beautiful. Are you a biker? I see you have traveled quite a bit. Have you made it to Iceland?"

- **The Dialogue.** After the first response, the conversation can continue and branch out into other areas of inquisitive exploration.

- **Personal Templating.** While we can write full responses to each individual prospective match from scratch, many daters have compiled paragraphs that they have used to question or respond to questions that can be copied and pasted into new correspondence. Clearly this procedure saves typing time, and it also eliminates the effort of creating something new and error checking it. But you do have to make certain that it is relevant to the prospective match. A perceptive reader will pick up the artifice and a potential match might be lost. Examples of the kinds of paragraphs you might consider for templating include:

- Personal histories – where we've lived and what we've done
- Educational experiences – areas of interest
- Careers – informal resumes and work experiences
- Family – growing up, parents, kids, grandkids
- Interests & hobbies
- What you're looking for
- Other things, as appropriate

- **Bulk Templating**. It is also possible to construct an entire message that is aimed at prospects who have one or more essential interests or characteristics. For instance, say you live in New Orleans, go to every LSU home football game, and love live jazz. Maybe you are only interested in dating someone who is similarly inclined. You may have also had the site filter for age, distance, religion, etc. Then you can examine each recommended match to see if they mention LSU and jazz any place in their profile. If they do, you send them a standard template:

> "I'm a huge LSU fan with season tickets to all of the home games. What do you think of the new coach? Do you tailgate?"
>
> "I'm also very into jazz. Have you been to Cubana Cielo in the Quarter?"
>
> "Tell me more about yourself."

According to Christian Rudder, cofounder of OKCupid, gifted data nerd, and author of <u>Dataclysm: Love, Sex, Race, and Identity--What Our Online Lives Tell Us about Our Offline Selves</u> [9.2], sending a generic message will typically be 75% as effective as a custom version. For more efficacy, we can customize it a bit for each recipient.

CHAPTER 9: THE PROFILE

It will probably come as no surprise that I have used this technique extensively because I am a Geek and because I have always attempted to juggle a significant number of matches simultaneously.

Traditional & Chance In-Person Meetings

As a result of having prepared for online dating, you may be more mentally and physically prepared to date others you meet during religious services, while pursuing your interests (sports, hobbies, arts, entertainment, etc.), at work, or people that you randomly bump into on the street. You now have questions for those you encounter, and you also have determined the answers to many of their potential questions.

Many people feel uncomfortable about formally dating, but those we happen to meet by chance actually offer us the opportunity to practice without pressure. We can engage in casual conversation without indicating any interest in dating them. In fact, speaking with others we aren't intending to date gives us the chance to try different approaches and get feedback without the fear of failing. At the very least, it helps us become more sociable and confident.

My Personal Experience with Filtering

I have not seen a filter on any site for "Occupation", but I was prejudiced against psychiatrists and psychologists and always deleted them. I never really knew any, but I guess I was concerned that they might be weird or want to stick pins in me. After all, they come up with these crazy questions like "Would you rather pull the wings off a butterfly or walk naked into a pep rally in the gym?"

Well, I got a "Like" and a message from one who was very engaging, so I responded, the whole time thinking, "Keep an open mind." I was in a FWB relationship that was suddenly to become exclusive the weekend this psychologist and I were to meet, so I called to cancel our "date". She suggested we "meet" anyway to see if we could just be friends. You guessed it, I fell head over heels in love, and I'm damn sure this is The One (the same one I mentioned before) – so far, so good.

BOOMERS OUT OF THE BOX

CHAPTER 10: SECURITY

SAFE DATING

Scams

Ever since man discovered rocks, society has been plagued with scammers. First it was cave-to-cave pushy pebble peddlers, followed by big rock candy mountain hustlers, and pet rock breeders. Once snail mail was established, scammers could focus on lonely men and women in a variety of confidence schemes. One such dating scam was derived from legitimate "mail order brides and grooms". The internet and digital data have led to an explosion of fraudulent schemes we struggle to avoid. Scammers can be enormously personable and credible performers with excellent accents and convincing stories. AI will make some of these scams even more compelling.

In general, there are two kinds of scams. They both involve misrepresentation:

- One is misrepresenting himself (or herself) to get a date. This could be a minor thing or could be the act of a person with ill intent.
- The other is hiding their true identity and/or location because they are trying to secure illicit financial gain at our expense. Most of these are from very remote sources, but some may actually show up and begin a relationship in person.

Red Flags

While they may be harmless, there are certain things people do or say that indicate they may not be truthful. When the flag appears, bring out the magnifying glass and investigate or flee. These are typical:

- No picture.
- Pictures that don't match the profile text.

- Catfishing: posting pictures that are just too good to be true.
- Written language which does not match the stated education level.
- Love bombing, which is being unrealistically complimentary or unjustifiably affectionate early in the process.
- Someone who is active on the computer/smart phone but stalls meeting on video or in person. They may be lying about their location – i.e. they are in a boiler room operation in Nigeria. They often misrepresent their indicated sex.
- Responses to questions that are evasive or don't address the questions you asked.[14]
- Overzealous communications soliciting immediate responses or moving too fast.
- A person who is manipulative or pushy.
- While many daters are members of more than one site, are they relatively consistent? If their profiles are significantly different, ask why?
- Someone who is giving you a weird vibe.

We need to consider potential problems if a red flag appears. If more than one flag occurs, that can be a strong warning. Trust your gut on this one.

Rules

While we may choose to interact with someone who creates a red flag, the following are safety rules and aren't discretionary:

- We should **never** give anyone our personal or financial information such as banking data, social security

---

[14] If you suspect a scam, ask location specific questions until you are certain they are real: "What grade school did you attend?" "What street did you live on?" "What are your favorite restaurants?"

CHAPTER 10: SECURITY

number, credit card number, passwords (for anything), or family details.

- Never send or accept money from anyone.
- Never carry (transport) a package for a match, even if they pay for travel expenses.
- Never send any photos or videos to a match that you wouldn't feel comfortable posting yourself on Facebook.
- Never go to an online dating site that hasn't been rated by several rating services. There are fake ones out there, and their purpose is to gain your personal data.

With 7 billion people on the planet, and a high percentage of sociopaths and others with criminal minds, crime directed against us is relentless. Technology provides incredible benefits for each of us personally and society as a whole, but it also provides the tools for thieves to rip us off. Remaining vigilant will help ensure that your computers, phones, finances, and bodies are safe and secure.

As added security and for peace of mind, once you get a person's full name and general address, you probably can find him or her with a Google search. LinkedIn and social media platforms are also good sources for confirmation.

SAFE TECH

The technical world has taken over the planet we used to know. It is impossible for any of us to make our systems totally safe. It's beyond the scope of this book (or any book) to eliminate all of the risk associated with our online lives, but this section will try to provide a few basics, keeping in mind that tech evolves quickly, and our responses to changes and unknown risks can lag significantly behind. If you don't have access to a tech guru or a precocious twelve-year-old, there are plenty of trustworthy websites to help guide you in improving the security of your computers and smart phones. The following are some first steps to employ:

- Keep software updates current. As annoying as the updating process can be, Apple, Microsoft, Google, and others do attempt to protect their platforms to the highest degree.

- Use strong and unique passwords. Generally, use a mix of upper- and lower-case letters, numbers, and special characters. Do not use any personal info like birthdates, address, names, etc. Don't use the same passwords on different accounts.

- Enable Two-Factor authentication. This is simple but requires taking an additional step when logging in.

- Select only apps that are secure. Check out reputable reviews of apps before downloading.

- Use anti-virus software. Many users employ a variety of security packages. Reviews are plentiful. Check out Forbes reviews for a start. [10.1]

- *Let your device help protect your data. iPhones and Android devices give you the option to prevent apps from knowing your precise location or accessing your entire photo library. Use these to your advantage. You may also have the option to tell apps not to track you as*

CHAPTER 10: SECURITY

you poke around on the web or in other apps, which can help safeguard your activity. [15]

- *Limit your exposure. Don't log in to your dating apps with your social media accounts, since this can give companies a way to access some of the information you've shared there. And resist the urge to respond to prompts from dating apps that encourage you to share more (and different kinds of) information.* [16]

---

[15] A Washington Post article by Chris Velazco entitled "Dating apps are collecting more of your information than you think" gives some DIY help and some food for thought. [10.2]
[16] IBID.

BOOMERS OUT OF THE BOX

CHAPTER 11: FORMAL DATING

"By failing to prepare, you're preparing to fail."
Benjamin Franklin

GET READY, 'CAUSE HERE IT COMES

"You have people come into your life shockingly and surprisingly. You have losses that you never thought you'd experience. You have rejection and you have [to] learn how to deal with that and how to get up the next day and go on with it."
Taylor Swift

While this chapter covers topics important for the first meeting, the meet-and-greet, general subjects applicable to later dating activity are also included.

Dating Goals

The next step is to establish goals for the meet-and-greet:

- Determining whether there is a feeling of positive chemistry and attraction.
- Deciding whether the body type, verbal style, and topics of conversational interest fit the profile of a person we want to meet again.
- Presenting ourselves effectively and honestly so that our dates will have the appropriate information to make an informed decision about whether they wish to date us.
- Asking for a more formal date if this first encounter was positive.

BOOMERS OUT OF THE BOX

Expectations for the Meet-and-Greet

Expectations we form while online and in telephone connections prior to a face-to-face meeting are necessarily frail. We tend to connect dots and then extrapolate to imagine the full person we are interested in. But we can't put much faith in these assumptions – there are way too many unknown variables. Therefore, reining in expectations tightly while keeping our minds open is likely to produce the most reliable results.

Where to Meet?

Based on the recommendations of most coaches, the venue for the meet-and-greet should be in a public place and in an environment that is easy, safe, and not loud. An inexpensive meal, coffee, or a walk in the park are typical choices. Movies can be fun, but the conversation is likely to be minimal and inefficient. Meet at a location that minimizes driving. Following dates can be more customized and creative.

Personal Presentation

"Ooh, baby, I love your way...."

Peter Frampton

First impressions are critical, and we only have one chance at it. If we botch it up, our potential relationship may become just a broken dream. People's standards for most things vary, and it is difficult to impossible to meet the highest in all categories. But success will smile more readily upon us when we are at our best.

The following checklist contains guidelines for all dating relationships. Some obvious items are included for a sense of completeness:

- Cleanliness is critical in everything about us and the spaces we control (home, car, etc.).
    - Our personal hygiene must assume the highest standards to avoid potential rejection. Of course, we all know to shower/bathe, brush our teeth,

CHAPTER 11: FORMAL DATING

and dress in clean clothes - regardless of the style.

- Less thought about, but important, is "hair control". Men especially have probably experienced hair loss, and to add insult to injury, annoying hair growth in different areas, such as the nose, ears, eyebrows, and facial hair that can mar a first impression. Women may find unwanted hair sprouting from their chins. (Men, additionally need to trim beards and mustaches and avoid stubble that can cause burns and deter passionate kissing later when more serious dating begins.)
- Fingernails must be clean to avoid rejection due to their appearance and trimmed smooth to prevent injury if and when the relationship advances to lovemaking.
- Natural body odor is an attraction to some people, but not to others. Fragrances designed to hide odor and/or attract a partner can backfire and repel them.[17] We need to use caution not to overdo it.

• Clothing style is a personal choice and tells part of the story of who we are. The dating venue will dictate general limitations, but we should wear clothes that enable us to feel confident, comfortable, and completely ourselves. While we are attempting to be as attractive as possible, we don't want to be over the top when we first meet. Many of our potential matches will be shy (about 50%) and/or introverted (about 33%), so it makes sense to tone things down at first – unless we want to eliminate that personality type quickly.

---

[17] According to Women's Voices for the Earth, "Almost 20% of the general population is sensitized to at least one allergen, and studies find that fragrance is one of the most frequently identified substances causing allergic reactions. Fragrance allergy affects 2 to 11 percent of the general population." [11.1]

BOOMERS OUT OF THE BOX

- Manners in the years before the 60's were rooted in chivalry, and men and women shared that expectation. Many, but definitely not all, women rejected men's traditional efforts as being inconsistent with their feminist viewpoints. While most agree with women's equality, it leaves chivalry in limbo. It seems reasonable and inoffensive if traditional manners are treated as the default until told otherwise. Good table manners and etiquette are always safe, while the lack thereof can be a potential deal breaker.
- Conversation is the mechanism through which the majority of information is shared. Our communication skills are important. For the greatest success, we can:
    - Exude confidence by smiling and maintaining eye contact.
    - Break a pattern that might start sounding like an interview by asking questions that follow a statement:
        - "I really enjoy documentaries; what kind of movies are your favorites?"
        - "I'm crazy about Italian food; what kind of food are you into?"
        - I just returned from a Mediterranean cruise; it was a blast. What kind of travel do you enjoy most?"
    - Make note of things like eye and hair color, clothing, and jewelry so we can offer a sincere compliment. We need to be sensitive when complimenting things that are transitory like fitness, figure, or looking youthful. Our potential partner may hear that if they don't maintain these physical qualities, the relationship may fail. Complimenting one's essence is pretty fail-safe:
        - "You are radiant."
        - "You have a glow or aura about you."

CHAPTER 11: FORMAL DATING

- "I love your energy."
- "You have beautiful eyes."

o When viewing midlife pictures, compliment with something like "What a great memory!" or "How wonderful a time!" but not "You were so cute then."

o Be present and listen attentively; focus on what is being said (and remember it) while asking questions you feel appropriate and in the context of the conversation. Simple examples:

- "You mentioned you have six children. Are they all in the area? Do you visit them often?"
- "Your profile states you love to travel. Where have you been? How often do you set off on an excursion? Where would you like to go in the coming years?"
- "You listed pickle ball as a sport you like. How often do you play?"
- "As you may have noted in my profile, I visit the Caribbean for a couple of weeks every winter to SCUBA dive. Does a vacation like that appeal to you?"
- "Do you like live music concerts? What kind of music?"

o Offer plenty of time for your date to speak and don't play one-upmanship by shifting your date's story to yourself.

o When it is your turn to speak, you do not want to be boastful or boring, but it is an opportunity to offer things about yourself that you feel are important to communicate. It also facilitates asking relevant questions. If you want to know where they grew up, you can first say where you grew up and then ask them.

- Discussion may include those topics identified earlier like desired relationship type, time available to commit, distance apart, etc. But first and foremost, you want it to be an interesting and enjoyable conversation and not like an interview for a position at the DMV.
- Be sensitive to boundaries or limitations on personal or intimate information. As a relationship progresses, and trust and confidence build, more private subjects can comfortably be explored.
- As things move along, perhaps a statement like this is appropriate, "I'm hoping to find a long-term relationship, but it takes time to be sure we're right together. In the meantime, I really like you and would like to continue dating. If it turns out not to work, at least we are having fun."
- Another approach might be, "I'm not ready for a long-term commitment, but it could happen at some point. Regardless, I really would like to continue seeing you."
- You also need to keep in mind that things change over time, so maintaining an open dialogue can ensure your partner will remain up to date and on board.

- Off limit subjects for early conversations include references to:
    - Weight – too risky to ever mention.
    - Former partners
        - You may discuss your past key relationships briefly and answer questions asked.
        - While some may want to hear past relationship details as insight into the prospective mate, others don't, so it is better to hold back unless asked. When

CHAPTER 11: FORMAL DATING

relating historical stories, it is best to use "I" instead of "we", such as "When I was in Paris...." rather than "When X and I were....".

- Dwelling on the loss of a partner can signal that you are not over the loss or that nobody will ever be able to replace them.
    o It's not helpful to mention the appearance or attractiveness of a particular member of the opposite sex – nobody wants to be compared to others.

- Baggage issues (emotional, legal, or financial), as discussed previously, travel with us throughout our lives. This is not the time for a heavy conversation about these elements unless it might be a deal breaker. Our profiles should have identified (explicitly or implicitly) important issues, but a more detailed explanation may be offered or requested.

- **Rejection is the norm and a necessary part of the process, not a symptom of personal failure or inadequacy. It's to everyone's advantage to fail quickly and allow both parties to move on.** It can hurt when someone we really wanted to date rejects us, but it is what it is. When the chemistry is not there, there's not anything anyone can do – we have no control over ours or theirs. The flip side is that we will be rejecting others, and that's not emotionally easy for most of us. It is always important to treat our would-be matches with respect. Ghosting (simply dropping out and never responding) is poor form and bad etiquette. If we really like someone but realize we don't have the chemistry, it can soften the blow to ask whether a friendship would be possible in the future. Other responses that are relatively gentle include:
    o "I've decided I'm really not ready to do anything at the moment."

- - "I've enjoyed meeting you. You are a lovely person, but just not the right one for me."
- Afterwards, review all of the interactions during the date, process the feedback, reflect on the whole event, and determine what you did well and what could use improvement or might need to be reevaluated. Decide whether you wish to continue seeing this match.

Dating is not a Reality Show

The Golden Batchelor (or Bachelorette) presents the premise that you can choose the best fit from 25 "contestants" and find wedded bliss. This assumes that the One will fall in love with one of the twenty-five, AND that all of the 25 are falling in love with the One. While this is clearly preposterous, that mindset can seep into online dating. Many individuals tend to focus on answering the question "**Which** of these great people I'm dating is the winner, the One?" Even though the answer could logically be "None", there can be a sense of urgency that some feel to get moving to start this new great life and just pick one. I'd suggest to you: FIGHT that instinct. If you find yourself picking this one over that one, you might want to hold off until you find one that doesn't leave you questioning. Being clear that this is The One can take time to ferret out. Meanwhile, try to enjoy the journey.

CHAPTER 11: FORMAL DATING

BOOMERS OUT OF THE BOX

CHAPTER 12: BUILDING RELATIONSHIPS

"Don't settle for a relationship that won't let you be yourself."

Oprah Winfrey

In a world of constant change, building and maintaining a relationship is forever a work in progress, not a destination. As seniors, over 90% of us have experience building relationships – for better or worse. Roughly half of all marriages end in divorce. According to Forbes, the average length of marriages in the US last 8 years, which is hardly "until death do us part".

BOOMERS OUT OF THE BOX

AS TIME GOES BY

*"Time, time, time
See what's become of me
While I looked around for my possibilities
I was so hard to please
But look around, leaves are brown
And the sky is a hazy shade of winter"*

A Hazy Shade of Winter
By Simon & Garfunkel

According to historian Stephanie Coontz, author of <u>The Way We Never Were: American Families and the Nostalgia Trap</u>, "Within the past 40 years, marriage has changed more than in the last 5,000." [12.2] Things were simpler (NOT BETTER) 5000 years ago when the concept of marriage first emerged to solidify a man's ownership of a woman or women. By the end of the 16th century, marriage agreements included the words "til death do we part", while the upper-class English male life expectancy was around 45. If the aristocratic couple married in their early to mid-20's, the results were typically around 20 years or less before the loss of one of the partners. The life expectancies of the lower classes were even shorter and so were their marriages. Today's life expectancies are near 80, yielding marriages lasting over 50 years, almost three times as long as when the vows were explicitly made for life.

People are complex, and relationships are complex squared. Perhaps we need to admit that commitments made as young adults should not be designed to bind us to a life sentence. We don't stop growing as individuals once married. With so many lifestyle options available, it is not surprising that couples' interests, desires, and plans diverge after the children are on their own. Let's hope we aren't carrying guilt around just because we have divorced.

The bottom line is that despite our experiences at relationship building, many of us have not mastered the tools to maintain them. Thus, maybe we should discuss and contemplate how

CHAPTER 12: BUILDING RELATIONSHIPS

to improve our relationship skills to allow us to joyfully live out our lives with a partner. Statistically, healthy (no chronic illnesses) couples that form at age 65 will, on average, have an expectation of less than 20 years before the death of one of the partners. Healthy 75-year-olds less than 9 years; 80-year-olds closer to 5 years.

Developing a New Perspective

Historically, many have believed that married partners were to provide everything for each other to complete them both – to satisfy every need. That could be a rational objective for couples of certain religions or cultures, but for most of us living in today's Western culture, this is not the situation. First, we all have many needs, wants, and desires; and it's hard to imagine any one person satisfying all of them. Second, to complicate the issue, our needs over the course of our lives can change dramatically. Contemporary relationships might best be formed around the expectations of unknown changes – physical, mental, and financial.

Relationship building for most of us in our early twenties was a reactive process because we didn't have a clue, and our expectations were more fantasy than reality. Through trial, error, and often silly dramas, we survived the gauntlet, and as we learned to compromise and become more sensitive to the differences between us, our relationships endured – or not. Hopefully, we are now wiser and have the capacity to relate and to compromise.

> *"Before you marry a person, you should first make them use a computer with slow internet service to see who they really are."*
>
> Will Ferrell

To build a meaningful relationship, we must continue to learn more about one another. We need to understand what makes our partners tick, or in some cases, tic. From profiles, early texting, and the beginning of formal dating, we are able to glean a general picture of the person we're attracted to, but we need to accumulate more detail. In addition to the "what's", like motivations, nuances, biases, beliefs, experiences, opinions, and tons more, we need to tune into the "how's", which might include:

- Are they quick to respond to situations that arise?
- Are they usually ready to engage in conversation, or do they hold back?
- How do they make decisions?
- How do they express their differences and resolve small conflicts?

The natural rhythm by which individuals move, work, accept change, etc. can differ greatly. Likewise, the urgency that potential partners assign to moving through the stages of forming this new relationship can vary significantly. Some of us, after having recently experienced a loss are overwhelmed and incapable of making rapid decisions or accepting major changes. Others of us may feel that time is slipping away as we age and desire to establish a relationship as soon as possible. Most of us are somewhere in between. It is important to discuss our intended timetables with a potential partner to foster agreement, compromise, or to call it quits and move on.

As we discussed earlier, an open mind and a willingness to compromise are essential on both sides to create a lasting relationship. This may be especially difficult for potential couples where one or both have lived independently for a significant amount of time. Partners must weigh the value of being in a relationship versus doing everything their own way. Believing that our point of view is universally right and held by any rational person will severely limit (or completely eliminate) the dating pool. One's not going to sell many MAGA hats in Berkeley.

Coming Clean – Avoiding a Future Disaster

Every lasting personal relationship of the heart relies on mutual trust and integrity, and it is important to be honest and forthright from the beginning. Not all of our prospects will present accurate full disclosures of themselves initially. Whether it's shaving a few years from their stated ages or omissions of unfavorable episodes from their pasts.

CHAPTER 12: BUILDING RELATIONSHIPS

Many Rom-Coms use these personal secrets as plot elements to introduce "entertaining" waves of drama that cause uncertainty in the viability of the new relationship when the truth (or partial truth) is ultimately revealed. To avoid this unforced error from causing a long-term dilemma, both parties can share an opportunity to fess up at a mutually agreed upon point early in the "courtship".

> *As I was thinking about this issue while dating a woman who I thought might be The One, I proposed that we set a date upon which we would disclose any material misstatements or untruths that we had (intentionally or unintentionally) written or spoken earlier or any secrets that have been withheld because of the fear of rejection. She agreed. I had nothing to disclose, but she offered that she was 5 years older than the age in the profile. All was well, so we continued with clear consciences. Had she said she was married or wanted to move to Alaska, it would have been a quick end to a relationship.*

Some disclosures can be deal-breakers, but if it's going to happen, it's much better to discover this before we invest a bunch of time. Other disclosures can be worked through as bygones without guilt.

BOOMERS OUT OF THE BOX

PERSONALITY

> " 'cause you got personality, Walk, with personality
> Talk, with personality, Smile, with personality
> Charm, with personality, Love, with personality
> And of Cause you've got A great big hea----art"
>
> Songwriters: Lloyd Price / Harold Logan

Along the way we can relate facts about our histories, experiences, and personal information, but we are, of course, much more than the data that would satisfy potential employers, application demanders, government form takers, and even online dating questionnaires. We are not just the pile of two-dimensional papers that chronicles our list of experiential debits and credits. We are complex three-dimensional sentient beings with integral personalities. We have capabilities, powers, hopes, dreams, emotions, fears, ambitions, needs, flaws, and so much more.

While mental health professionals can explore the practical details of our subconscious selves and do psychological profiles and other in-depth analyses, most of us, with some targeted contemplation, can subjectively and adequately, identify much about our own personalities. Basically, we can pose questions and answer them. We are not talking about psychology questions like: "Would you rather eat roadkill or pull the wings off of a butterfly?", although Myers-Briggs offers a gold standard test to determine into which of 16 psychological types a subject falls. The results of the M-B evaluation may be useful but introduce complexity and nuance that very often requires professional interpretation. There are numerous providers of this type of testing and analysis, many of which are online, but it is not necessary to purchase said services to identify and validate our own traits from our own perspectives. There are no right or wrong answers when reporting what we see and feel.

The purpose of the following exercise is **to gain a better understanding of yourself** which will help you to see where you sit relative to the personality features of a potential partner. With some traits, we will benefit from similarities, and in others we may find complimentary traits advantageous.

The questions below are categorically similar to tests used by some psychologists and automated programs like the one used by eharmony to profile our personality traits, but the results here are directly determined by subjective evaluation. In fact, after getting to know your match, it may be useful to sit down together and discuss where each of you falls on the various scales.

Personal Traits

Are you self-motivated and driven? Do you have a strong inner energy that powers you to do things? Are you the one who initiates the activities? Or do you follow the lead of others, feel comfortable just staying home, prefer to be more laid back, and/or are satisfied going with the flow? If both are too laid back, life may become boring and uneventful. *("What do you want to do?" "I don't know, what do you want to do?")*. If both are driven, time demands and unrelated activities may create conflict, but alternatively, partners may often enjoy pursuing interests separately on their own. If one is driven and the other not, this can work well if the laid-back member is happy being "chauffeured".

Laid-Back---Driven

Are you controlling? Must you be in charge, or are you happier not being saddled with responsibility? Do you prefer to follow the lead of a partner you trust? In this context, control is obvious and direct. Decisions are made transparently. Roles are formally or tacitly accepted. Opposites in this area may work well together. Two strong controlling personalities might not play well together. Efforts to control the other's behavior or responses that are done indirectly or deceitfully are manipulative and neither healthy nor desirable.

Submissive------------------------------------Controlling

BOOMERS OUT OF THE BOX

Do you maintain a positive attitude? Are you usually pleasant towards new ideas, changes, and possibilities or are you negative under the assumption that you are being realistic? Do you often worry or feel helpless? Life is typically more pleasant for couples with positive attitudes, but a balance may yield better decision making as the pros and cons get hashed out.

Negative/Half Empty------------------Positive/Half Full

Do you tend to withdraw under pressure? Do you retreat from potential disagreement or conflict, or are you assertive and face things straight on? Both partners who are similar at the more extreme ends of the spectrum can find themselves either ignoring problems until it's too late or constantly arguing. More central positions often work best here.

Avoid---Confront

Are you conventional? Are you traditional and conservative in your approach to life and problem solving or are you more unconventional with a tendency to think creatively? Are you predictable or are you full of surprises? Balance without extremes can work here but so can partners who are similar in this regard.

Traditional/predictable----------Unconventional/Creative

Do you have a need for structure? Do you require a great deal of organization, or do you tend to be more organic and free form? Extreme opposites in this area can be very annoying to one another.

Loosely Structured-------------------------Super Organized

Do you have a need for adventure? Do you get bored easily and seek out new and unusual experiences, or do you tend to hold back or participate in more sedentary activities? Opposites may suffer in the togetherness department having difficulty finding experiences to share that appeal to both of them.

Tentative---Adventurous

CHAPTER 12: BUILDING RELATIONSHIPS

Social

Are you introverted or extroverted? Are you shy, timid, or withdrawn versus outgoing and gregarious? If shy or introverted, do you wish to have someone to assist you in engagement, or do you prefer to be left on your own?

Introverted---Extroverted

Are you very social? Do you frequently engage in social activities, or do you prefer solo endeavors?

Solo---Social

Relationships

Do you seek closeness in your relationship? Do you want to share your feelings, thoughts, and daily experiences when together? Or do you prefer emotional privacy, parallel play, and quiet time when together? Similar responses from partners bode well.

Less Attached--Close

How much togetherness do you desire? Do you wish to spend most or all your time together when you can, or do you prefer a significant amount of time alone? Again, similar responses from partners bode well.

Alone---Together

Are you empathetic to your partner's feelings? Do you listen carefully, and are you sensitive in your reactions? Can you understand another's perspective and feel what they feel? The more empathy in a relationship, the better.

Less Empathetic-------------------------------------Empathetic

Are you adaptable? Are your habits and behavior patterns flexible or rigid? Are you willing and able to adapt as required to accommodate the needs or requests of others? Or do you tend to be rigid with a reluctance to defer? Due to their lack of capacity to compromise or give in, partnerships with two inflexible individuals can be at loggerheads if their views on most topics aren't very similar

Rigid---Adaptable

BOOMERS OUT OF THE BOX

Are you generous? Do you share your time, effort, or treasure with those you deem worthy? Do you give of yourself to a partner? Or do you tend to be selfish, tight, or stingy with your good will? Do you withhold in hopes that others will step up? Or are you possibly just out of touch with the needs of others?

Not So Generous---------------------------Very Generous

Do you tend to compensate? Do you attempt to offset a lack of something in your character by providing excesses in other areas? Do you shower a partner with gifts to make up for all of the times you are away pursuing your own interests? If one or both partners feel the scale is unbalanced, contention can ensue.

None------------------------------------Over Compensation

Do you have a strong desire for domesticity? Do you want to be engaged in taking care of the home and family, or would you prefer that your partner assumes that role? When neither partner accepts the domestic responsibility, working out a formula for sharing the load will be essential.

Not Domestic----------------------------------Very Domestic

Are you an open communicator? Do you speak freely and transparently or are you reserved and opaque or indirect when you communicate? Are you verbally forthcoming or are you guarded and defensive? While you know that good communication is necessary for successful relationships, communication that is primarily negative, nagging, or complaining can be harmful.

Guarded/Defensive---------------------Open/Transparent

How do you make decisions? Decisions can be made from the more automated (survival) part of the brain, which is instinctive, reactive, and heavily influenced by emotion & feelings, or by the more reasoned part of the brain which is governed by intellect & contemplation. Individuals differ across the spectrum from total reliance on feelings to exclusively using logic and reasoning. The majority of us use a mix depending on the situation. Couples who are on the extreme

CHAPTER 12: BUILDING RELATIONSHIPS

opposite ends of the continuum can have a major challenge in terms of reconciling differences. They can experience stress, disagreement, and/or conflict when their methods collide, but when both feelings and logic are combined, decisions can be more solid.[18]

Emotion -------------------------------------Reason/Logic

The self-assessment is a subjective scale and not an exact science. In fact, it can be very distorted simply because it is subjective and far from an exact science. Note also that you may not know enough about the person with whom you are comparing yourself. Everyone perceives things differently. Gender alone can be an important factor.

There are thousands of possible points of differences between yourself and your potential partner. Clearly, there is never an absolutely perfect match.

> "Don't let the perfect be the enemy of the good."
>
> Attributed to Voltaire

It can be both fun and instructive to sit down after several dates and together answer the questions with your potential partner. The discussion is likely to be more interesting than the answers.

---

[18] For a comprehensive discussion covering reflexive (immediate reaction) vs reflective (taking a moment to reason), see [12.1].)

BOOMERS OUT OF THE BOX

RECOGNIZING OUR DIFFERENCES
Too much or just right, that is the question.

Figure 11. Don't let a few differences ruin a match.

CHAPTER 12: BUILDING RELATIONSHIPS

They say opposites attract, and we have all seen examples of such relationships. While the dating of opposites can be interesting, intriguing, and intoxicating initially, the relationship may become difficult to hold together in the long run if the differences are too great. The amusing can become the annoying. Cute might morph into conflict. OR NOT! It often takes open, accepting minds and a concerted effort to bridge some of the contrasts.

Every couple has differences, and it's important to flesh them out while dating. The big items (say religion, sexual practices, politics, etc.) are obvious and high priority, but the smaller conflicting items also need to be uncovered, and significant time together is necessary for this to occur. In addressing the issues, there is no substitute for honest direct discussion and resolution. Try this NY Times link to flesh out differences: "The 36 Questions That Lead to Love". [L.11]

COMPROMISE

Basically, we don't want to sweat the small stuff, and most things are small stuff. In the bigger scheme of life, the majority of our little differences are just not worth fretting about. It's important to put these issues into the proper perspectives. It's far better to create a win-win scenario through discussion and compromise than to devolve into a contest of wills battling for primacy. We can be far happier if we can get over the small annoyances and move on to the important opportunities - to have fun and give pleasure to ourselves and those we love.

Before even discussing compromises or other solutions, it's important to understand a partner's point of view. A good place to start is to ask: "Can you help me understand…? Would you please walk me through how you came to that conclusion?" When we can better understand each other's positions, a win-win solution may be formulated. If not, then compromise may be required.

There are multiple ways to structure compromise. As an example, take a disagreement over a one-month vacation that one partner wants to spend in Italy versus the other's desire to go to Japan. There are several potential paths to compromise available to address this problem:

- Split the time so that each trip is two weeks. This gives each 50% of what they wanted, or from another perspective, 100% of what they wanted for half the time.

- Do Italy this year, and Japan next (or vice versa). This gives each 100% of what they wanted, but one party must delay gratification.

- Take separate vacations. Both get to go and do what they wish, but they go alone.

- Hybrid. Variations of the above solutions adding other conditions that balance out any critical details for one or both parties.

CHAPTER 12: BUILDING RELATIONSHIPS

EMOTIONAL INTELLIGENCE

As our life experiences in relationships clearly show, there can be significant differences in the way men and women respond to situations, interact, and handle issues. The book by John Gray, <u>Men Are from Mars, Women Are from Venus</u>, [12.3] describes the problem-solving orientation of most males versus the feelings-based attitudes of most females. This is an excellent starting point, and a fun read, for gaining critical insight into interaction between the sexes.

> *As Dr Shawn Andrews, leadership and EQ [emotional quotient] coach, aptly put it: "Boys are socialized very early on to be competitive, confident, assertive, decisive and even aggressive. Boys are taught about hierarchy, and that winning is the most important thing. Girls receive very different messages in their childhoods. Girls are socialized to be nurturing, care about others, show emotions, get along and be empathetic. Girls learn that the process is more important than winning and that relationships are key." [12.4]*

The study of "emotional intelligence", popularized by Psychologist Daniel Goleman, can be positively transformational for people. The term encompasses:

- Self-awareness: Recognizing one's strengths and weaknesses and being in touch with one's feelings and emotions.

- Self-regulation: Developing the capability to consciously regulate one's moods and emotional responses rather than being buffeted about by feelings.

- Motivation: Maintaining a positive outlook on life, a sense of purpose, and strong relationships with family and friends.

- Empathy: Understanding and compassionately relating to the emotions and experiences of others and developing social skills, such as reading facial expressions, body language, actions, voices, and other indicators to interpret moods, thoughts, and the feelings of other people.

Men and women who develop high degrees of emotional intelligence possess the tools necessary to understand the innate and conditioned characteristics of the opposite sex so they can more easily form working relationships. A Google search on emotional intelligence books, tests, and podcasts will return more links than any of us have time to explore. You can check a couple of links out and decide upon a course of action that meets your needs.[19]

---

[19] Michael Clayton – Introduction to emotional intelligence oriented toward work and management [L.9]

Joshua Freedman, Six Seconds, "What Is the Definition of Emotional Intelligence?" [L.10]

CHAPTER 12: BUILDING RELATIONSHIPS

COMMUNICATIONS

"Assumptions are the termites of relationships."

Henry Winkler

Good communication is essential in order to attain our goals and develop sustainable relationships. Since we come from a variety of backgrounds, experiences, and past relationships, we cannot assume we have a common knowledge or understanding with a potential partner. Just as every pilot knows, miscommunication with air traffic control can lead to accidents; misunderstanding one another can damage or ruin relationships.

Libraries are full of worthy books on personal communications for DIY enthusiasts. The internet can provide thousands of articles, podcasts, and social media entries. Many psychologists, couples' therapists, and dating coaches build their practices around the subject. Communication is extremely important and a common issue in all forms of relationships. So, let's discuss how to avoid miscommunication.

Will a possible match misinterpret your messages due to likely assumptions or implications? Is it likely that a match might assume that you still ski because you showed a picture of yourself on skis? Did you imply that you enjoy leisure travel when you messaged a potential partner that their picture of the Eiffel Tower reminded you of the good times you've had in Paris?

Sometimes you might sense from a partner's response that you may not have been understood correctly, so it's a good idea to restate your thought in a different way to clear any potential ambiguities. Active listening (listening attentively and reflecting back to the speaker to confirm what was said) can help detect messaging gone astray.

Confirmed Dialogue

Active listening is standard practice in radio communications. To take another simple example from aviation:

BOOMERS OUT OF THE BOX

Robin 56: Sacramento Air Traffic Control, this is Robin 56 requesting descent to McClellan.

SATC: Roger Robin 56, You are cleared descent to 8500 feet.

Robin 56: Roger, cleared to 8500 feet.

To avoid misunderstandings, communication was confirmed by Robin 56 who repeated the information back to the controller. Note: Unlike conversations among couples, Air Traffic Control communications are recorded in order to assign blame later. (*It does make one wonder what the effect might be on couples if all conversations were somehow recorded!*)

Speaking requires:

- Facing the listener,
- Enunciating at a reasonable volume, and
- Monitoring visual responses for signs of understanding.

Listening requires:

- Attention, demonstrated by eye contact and body language,
- Ability to hear and process what is being said, and
- Accurate interpretation of the gestures and expressions accompanying the words.

It is important to acknowledge any physical deficiencies and take corrective action. On the one hand, we all know a friend or family member who mumbles, speaks very softly, or tries to talk to us from another room or facing away from us. On the other hand, we also know those who can't hear and refuse to get hearing aids. Both hearing and eyesight degrade over time. Living in denial is annoying to those around us and leads to isolation when we can't engage in meaningful conversation while repeating "what?" constantly or giving up and tuning out.[20]

---

[20] Saturday Night Live did a great parody of elderly use of Amazon Echo. Search "Amazon Echo SNL" for the video vignette.

CHAPTER 12: BUILDING RELATIONSHIPS

Understanding

Successful communications require both clear transmission **and** correct reception. If either is missing or inaccurate, failure results. If this becomes a pattern, the relationship will suffer greatly. Established habits that worked well enough with a previous partner may not suffice with a new one.

Note that the precision used in word selection demonstrated by a prospective partner may be quite different from our own. Someone who is very literal can become confused if we are more carefree or careless in our language – interjecting humor, sarcasm, or atypical word selection. Others get lost if the subject of discussion is suddenly changed without warning. Cultural or regional language patterns, accents, and vocabulary can also form obstacles to successful communication. Be sensitive to how your messages are received. It's a good idea to stop and correct or explain anything that seems like it might have been misinterpreted. When on the receiving end of the discussion, periodically summarizing what you have understood thus far can mitigate any doubt or potential confusion.

If you are using humor, and if it becomes clear that it has fallen flat or been taken seriously, it makes sense to immediately apologize and explain that you were just trying to be funny. Defending a miscalculation usually just exacerbates the problem. Humor is context sensitive and requires us to know our audience. This can take time in a new relationship, although different senses of humor could indicate a poor long-term match.

Feedback

There is a whole world of things to talk about, and we all benefit by sharing discoveries and thoughts relating to interesting topics with a partner. Most importantly, however, closeness and intimacy are formed by sharing feelings in an ongoing way. We don't want to hold things back until we explode as we proceed in life together. Feedback acts as a relief valve and can lead to important changes in a new relationship resulting in greater satisfaction and comfort for

BOOMERS OUT OF THE BOX

both people. Examples of the kinds of things to discuss include:

- Activities such as attending religious services, watching football, taking yoga classes, etc. may not be fun or tolerable for one partner. It's best to share feelings, likes, dislikes, preferences, etc. early on.

- Daily routines feel comforting to many, but we each have personal preferences that could be out of sync with a partner's. Steadfast morning people matched with night people will most likely need to talk – maybe a lot! Issues like regular times for fitness, health, naps, reading, work, etc. can evoke discussion and sharing of opinions and feelings.

- Environmental comfort is critical, and rather than grinning and bearing it, we can express our feelings. Mutual feedback can bring the issue to the forefront and lead to compromise, rather than thermostat wars.

- Food requirements or preferences are pervasive issues in our culture today. Vegetarian, glutton-free, weight control, muscle building, organic, and a host of specialized diets can create complexity in meal preparation. While it is recommended that we keep an open mind and try new things, it's important to express feelings about food choices routinely. It can also be quite important to some to share the cooking. This can mean cooking together or alternating the responsibility in some way. Likewise, even cleanup can be accomplished by the one who did not cook or some other agreement.

- Orderliness and the need for organization vary considerably from person to person. Good things can happen when feedback is provided that leads to a positive discussion and compromise, thereby preventing the development of unnecessary stress.

- As issues arise and strained feelings emerge, calm communication is even more important. One of the best approaches is to ask, "**Do you want to be helped,**

CHAPTER 12: BUILDING RELATIONSHIPS

heard or hugged?" Automatically attempting to solve the problem without first finding out what your partner is looking for, may actually work against resolution.

- Sleeping together (actually sleeping) is often problematic if one partner snores, is restless, gets up frequently, or has sleep apnea. In such cases – which are common - separate bedrooms (or at least two beds) may provide the best solution.

As stated before, these are merely representative examples of a myriad of potential issues. While the details differ, the process remains the same: share your feelings and requests with your partner in an attempt to resolve the differences.

Not all forms of feedback are welcomed. But whenever possible, stating the positive, what you would like, as opposed to negative, a criticism or what you don't want, is likely to be better received and less likely to lead to a defensive response. Also, repetitive feedback may be experienced as nagging, which can be annoying and counterproductive. A reasonable balance is called for.

INTIMACY

The State of Having a Close Relationship and Connection with Someone - Physical, Emotional, and/or Personal

Intimacy is at the core of relationship building. It is essential. Having sex may be physically intimate, but true intimacy is so much more. The depth and richness of an intimate relationship is the reason we are spending time and effort seeking The One. The following quotations describe elements of intimacy better than I can, so I offer them for consideration:

> *"Intimacy transcends the physical. It is a feeling of closeness that isn't about proximity but of belonging. It is a beautiful emotional space in which two become one."*
> Steve Maraboli

> *"If you age with somebody, you go through so many roles – you're lovers, friends, enemies, colleagues, strangers; you're brother and sister. That's what intimacy is if you're with your soulmate."*
> Cate Blanchett

> *"Passion is the quickest to develop, and the quickest to fade. Intimacy develops more slowly, and commitment more gradually still."*
> Robert Sternberg

> *"Those who have never known the deep intimacy and the intense companionship of mutual love have missed the best thing that life has to give."*
> Bertrand Russell

> *"Intimacy is not purely physical. It's the act of connecting with someone so deeply, you feel like you can see into their soul."*
> Reshall Varsos

The sharing of ourselves is at the core of intimacy. Although there is a certain degree of sharing our bits and bodily fluids,

CHAPTER 12: BUILDING RELATIONSHIPS

sex alone does not demand full intimacy. Likewise, intimacy does not require sex. Intimacy of any sort comes with shared vulnerability and requires mutual trust and respect.

BOOMERS OUT OF THE BOX

PART: 3 SEX & AGING

Figure 12. Aging may make sex a blur, but it can still be great.

BOOMERS OUT OF THE BOX

CHAPTER 13: SEX & THE MODERN SENIOR

"Good sex is like good bridge. If you don't have a good partner, you'd better have a good hand."

Mae West

Sex may have been removed from your list of desirable activities, and there may certainly be solid reasons for this decision. Nonetheless, I strongly recommend that you read this chapter to reconsider the possibility of revisiting the opportunity for pleasure and intimacy.

REALITIES OF SENIOR SEX

Many of us are shocked at the person we see when we look in the mirror. "Who is that? How can this be? I don't feel that old!" Well, reality can be terrifying! While it hits us all at different rates, physical and mental decline visits us all. *On average, we reach our sexual peak in our 20s, our physical peak in our 30s, our mental peak in our 40s and 50s, and are happiest and most relaxed in our 60s.* [13.1] Even with the natural progression of diminished capabilities, we still can accommodate and function sexually.

Sex should NOT be painful for a woman. Many issues are correctable and/or treatable.

Vaginal senility or atrophy is a condition of thinning in the vaginal walls that leads to small tears, inflammation, and pain during sex. It is most common in women who have not had sex for a prolonged period. While it falls under the category of "use it or lose it", it is typically reversible in a short period of time. Check out this 2nd Act TV video on YouTube. [13.3] See a Mel Robbins Podcast [13.2] that presents an excellent discussion of a full range on vaginal subjects and is guaranteed to be enlightening.

According to the Healthy Aging Poll:

- *While 46 percent of seniors aged 65 to 70 report being sexually active, that number decreases to 25 percent for those 76 and over.*

- *More senior men report being sexually active than women, at 51 percent compared to 31 percent. [Note that many senior men are married to younger women and that there are nearly twice as many single senior women than men.]*

- *Seniors who reported their health as "fair" or "poor" were 23 percent less likely to report being sexually active than those who reported their health as "excellent" or "good."*

CHAPTER 13: SEX AND THE MODERN SENIOR

- *76 percent of [sexually active] seniors aged 65 to 80 agree that sex is an important part of their relationship.*
- *Nearly 3 in 4 seniors report being satisfied with their sex life, though women were 8 percent more likely to report this than men.*
- *Among seniors, 18 percent of men and 3 percent of women take a medication or supplement related to their sexual function.* [13.4]

The figures quoted above are sufficient to conclude that sex is still important to the majority of Boomers and is worthy of significant attention. Nonetheless, many feel as though they have aged out of sexual activities and consider that a normal progression. But before you abandon the concept of a grand sex life, you may want to contemplate the answers to a few questions. This same list may be useful in part to open a sexual dialogue with a partner:

- What is your actual sexual experience based on?
    - How many sexual partners have you had? Some of us have only had a single partner, while others have had many. The more lovers we've had, the more skills and varied experiences we are likely to have acquired. Nonetheless, there is still so much more we can learn if we are adventurous and open-minded.
    - What is the range of the sexual activity you have engaged in? While some of us may have sampled a wide variety of sexual options, most have not. This can be an opportune time to investigate and consider new possibilities and activities with new partners. If it feels good, do it! What's the downside? If you don't enjoy it, you can stop.
    - What experiences have you found truly pleasurable or totally unenjoyable? Fully describe and share these preferences and boundaries together with your new partner.

- - o How frequently do you orgasm and in what situations? Sex is certainly more than just orgasm, but it is a highly pleasurable part of sex that is not experienced by everyone. See the section "ORGASM: AN EXPERIENCE OF CLIMAX IN SEXUAL PLEASURE" in the following chapter.
  - Are you shy or embarrassed by your body? While many of us do try to keep fit, our bodies are simply not what they used to be. We therefore need to cut ourselves (and our lovers) some slack. We are likely to be a lot happier[21] if we lower our expectations and accept the reality that we are no longer the young, buff, glamorous image the media use to promote whatever they are selling. We are each attractive and sexy in our own ways.

Some have found that viewing regular people in the nude can help us to be more accepting of our own naked bodies. HBO's "Naked Attraction" series offers a potpourri of nude body types in a dating game format. If you can endure a half dozen or so seasons of the show, you will probably emerge with considerably more confidence in your own body. Likewise, visiting a nudist camp or clothes free venue can reduce inhibitions and build confidence. It may be terrifying to think about it initially, but most who try it find it incredibly liberating and a fun adventure to take with a friend or friends.

- How long has it been since you've been in a sexual relationship? If it has been years since you've had sex, you may be more anxious about renewing the activity. You may also be remembering past experiences with your younger body and younger partners. To embark upon a new sexual adventure, it's important to lower your performance expectations for orgasms or erections while keeping an open mind to the

---

[21] See 2nd Act TV for a meaningful discussion of body and intimacy concerns. [13.5]

CHAPTER 13: SEX AND THE MODERN SENIOR

pleasurable possibilities offered by a new partner and maybe even new forms of love making.

- Do you suffer from erectile dysfunction, vaginal dryness/pain, or performance anxiety? Most Boomers have anxieties that reduce performance and/or enjoyment in one way or another during sex, especially if they are continuing to follow the same routines they have used for decades. Adjustments in activities and patterns can serve us well if we use lubricants to compensate for dryness and pills, pumps, and/or injections for ED. Likewise, we can substitute skilled cunnilingus, fellatio, and sex toys for full penetration.[22]

- Are you able to successfully masturbate? It is important to many of us to have some solo time. It is also useful to be able to achieve a release or pleasure ourselves when a partner is not available, tired, or "not in the mood". Couple masturbation can be both enjoyable and instructive in showing a partner how to pleasure us, and learn how to pleasure him or her.

- What are the sexual fantasies you would seriously desire to fulfill? Fantasies can be very simple (fascination with lingerie) to elaborate (being seduced by Batman or Barbie). It's whatever you want it to be, but unlikely to be fulfilled without sharing your wishes with your lovers.

Studies show that seniors looking back on their lives regret the things they wanted to do, but did not, far more than the things

---

[22] According to Cosmopolitan, relating to women over 60:
"...often includes embracing the fact that 'sex doesn't mean penile penetration,'.... 'As time goes on, people are redefining sexuality in terms of what they do and who they do it with. For a lot of couples, they acknowledge the fact that the male partner can't maintain an erection and she may have vaginal dryness, so they do mutual masturbation, oral sex, and manual stimulation.'"
[Self-reported:] "...respondents report that age has had no negative impact on the quality of their orgasms—in fact, 20 percent report orgasms that are more satisfying than ever before. Better yet, 57 percent say they reach climax with their partners always or almost always, suggesting we've gotten damn good at letting our lovers know what works." [13.6]

BOOMERS OUT OF THE BOX

they did that didn't work out. If you're trying to build a new romantic relationship, sex is a major component that you can redesign from scratch with a new partner to better satisfy your current shared desires and physical limitations. Sexual norms from decades ago have evolved significantly, and more options are available than ever before. So, you might want to keep an open mind. **This phase of your life can offer a period of sexual enjoyment and freedom that you may never have had time or opportunity for while you were younger.**

SEXUAL EXPLORATION & COMMUNICATION

Sexual Subjects to Discuss

For most of us, a conversation about sex with a new (or even an existing) partner can be awkward and difficult to initiate, but it is essential that this discussion takes place, not just at the beginning, but throughout the relationship, in order for sex to remain satisfying.

- **Potential sex related activities and their limits.** Touch, oral, anal, intercourse, fetishes, BDSM (bondage, discipline, sadism, & masochism), DS (dominance & submission), groups, or other? Manual and oral stimulation can lead to more orgasmic sex than intercourse for some of us. If any of the kinkier alternatives strike a positive chord, there are options for couples to engage in them incrementally. These conversations have been found by some to be easier to initiate by talking about what they are NOT into. Starting at this extreme point, is more likely to elicit agreement, possibly leading to one partner offering something else that's off the table. This brief "not that" conversation can evolve into "have you ever?" or "would you ever?" to "I think I would like to try that."

- **Clothing.** Come as you are, sexy outfit, lingerie, themed costume (cosplay), or nude? Clothing can be a major element of foreplay for many people. Some feel attire that is layered or partially revealing is sexier and more stimulating than nudity. The striptease is based upon anticipation that grows as articles are removed. Excitement can build in a similar way as a partner's clothing is removed. Costumes can trigger fantasies and introduce playfulness that is exciting. Others prefer to be nude as soon as possible.

- **Exhibitionism.** Where are you on the spectrum of total modesty vs. nude performer? In the animal kingdom, of which we are a part, many creatures exist as a result of the exhibition by one partner in order to attract another. It can be a beautiful body, a dance, a color, a song, a smell, feathers, etc. In humans, it can be many of these. Women are generally, but not exclusively, more inclined to dress, groom, walk, dance, etc. more provocatively when attempting to communicate their availability and desire than men, who are typically (but not universally) more reserved. Some men tend to exhibit their fitness, prowess, and financial success in attempts to attract the attention of women.

- **Foreplay.** Foreplay is the mental and physical activity engaged in to generate arousal in both partners before intercourse and other activities potentially leading to orgasm. Kissing of all sorts is a fire starter, but what other forms do you or would you like to engage in: dancing, stripping, watching porn, touching, role playing, etc.? Dirty talk, telling an erotic story, or reading aloud romance novel type material can be a powerful way to set the mood. As we age, new limitations make intercourse for either the man or the woman impossible or painful, so **foreplay becomes THE sex act**, and it can be immensely pleasurable and rewarding in and of itself.

- **Location.** In the movies, sex appears explosive and takes place anywhere. But where do you prefer to make love: in bed, against a wall, on the floor, on a table, in a chair, on a Tantric chair, in a car, out in the yard, in a pool, in a public area, etc.? While sex has been performed everywhere imaginable, comfort favors a relatively soft, right sized horizontal surface – AKA a bed. But there are times when an empty bed is not available, but a pool table or an airplane lavatory is. While a beach might be preferred over a tile floor, it is important to keep in mind that abrasive sand is a real issue!

- **Mood Makers.** Remember the importance of mood makers which include lighting, music, marijuana,

CHAPTER 13: SEX AND THE MODERN SENIOR

candles, and fragrance. Alcohol can improve the mood but in quantity can impede performance.

Detailed Feedback

Ask not only what your partner can do for you – ask what you can do for your partner.

It is important to share, show, and train a partner in terms of what we like and want:

- Share your preferences for those activities and actions which bring you pleasure.
- Show through demonstration what to do and how to make the experience pleasurable.
- Use feedback to train (and be trained by) a partner in the art of providing and attaining optimum pleasure.

Review each liaison from both perspectives after completing. While it might not be worth the effort to engage in a "How was it for you?" after a hookup, it is certainly worth it for any serious relationship. A simple "Great!" is not the goal. Honest and complete feedback is needed to improve the experience to the highest degree.

Verbal requests during lovemaking to do or perform something. Say "yes" to the greatest extent possible and within your boundaries when invited to participate in a specific act of love making. Meeting these requests affords you the opportunity to bring joy to your lover, potentially discover some new pleasures, and receive feedback that can improve your connection. Discussion during lovemaking is necessary to train and learn how to maximize pleasure for the both of you. You can't expect your partners to know what you're thinking or wanting.

Physically guiding or directing your partner in terms of position (body, hands, tongue, penis, etc.). Additional real-time feedback for speed, firmness, pressure, duration, direction ("higher", "lower", "to the left"), lubrication, etc. allows you to more effectively bring greater pleasure to a partner.

BOOMERS OUT OF THE BOX

Laughter as a part of lovemaking. Love and lovemaking are serious subjects, but laughter can definitely be part of the equation. As we talk about communication, it's important not to ignore the emotional value of joy and spontaneous outbursts of laughter and play on our mental wellbeing. As frustrating as *coitus interruptus* can be, it can also be quite humorous when a leg gets caught in the sheets or the doorbell rings. Laughter is an enhancer, an elixir to complement a cherished event.

Experimentation

"If you obey all the rules you miss all the fun."

Katharine Hepburn

Learning and growth require envisioning things differently than we have before. Testing new possibilities is part of the process. Minor explorations may lead to major adventures. But an open mind is the gateway to change, whether it's an extension of current knowledge or out-of-the-box thinking.

It is highly recommended that new acts, methods, or activities be thoroughly discussed before actually attempting them to avoid confusion and blame being placed for an experiment that backfires.

- **Sex toys.** Have you tried vibrators, rabbits, Kegel weights, Sybian saddles, electric wands, Womanizer (vacuum clitoris stimulators), dildos, cock rings, butt plugs, Eroscillator, etc.? Sex aids or enhancers can improve pleasure measurably when used solo or as a couple. While some of us may find toys over the top, most don't, and the range of choices is such that almost any couple can find something fun and pleasurable. Post-menopausal women often find that it requires more time to reach the arousal stage and that additional stimulation from various toys can shorten that period. Vibrators are the most common devices used and a good place to start. Visiting a sex shop with a partner to see the array of toys and games can be an adventure and a great introduction to a whole new world for some. Amazon is also always available for browsing. Good Vibrations (Goodvibes.com and its brick-and-mortar

CHAPTER 13: SEX AND THE MODERN SENIOR

stores) is a sex-positive, shame-free, woman-friendly place to shop for all things pleasure.

- **Sex games.** Cards, board games, dice, truth or dare, twister, spin the bottle, etc. abound. There are a bevy of games targeting groups and individual couples. Their purpose is to combine entertainment and adventure with expanded sexual experiences. Some are designed to overcome inhibitions such as nudity via something like strip poker. Twister, card/dice games with sex act descriptions, and truth or dare type games can be used as foreplay or to go all the way. Many of the games target small groups (parties and swingers) to foster intercouple or voyeur sex. With just a bit of ingenuity almost all existing games can be modified to include sexual entertainment for one or more couples. Don't knock "Go Fish" until you've tried it with adult rules.

- **Sex clubs.** Clubs created for exploring sexual activities are estimated to number around 3,000 in the US, but most are not advertised. These private clubs vary considerably and may serve as a platform for pursuing fetishes, BDSM, pole dancing, and different types of sexual play. They may also be aimed at swingers with rooms for couples or groups that may be private or public. Clothing may be optional, and voyeurs are usually welcome to help fulfill the needs of the exhibitionists. Some sex clubs are designed for couples and singles to attend together, but it can be less intimidating for first timers to bring a friend and enter as a couple.

- **Swinging.** Formally swapping sexual partners among couples at parties and swing events is estimated to be practiced by 2-5% of the US adult population. Hookups might be between two couples who meet at a bar or within a large group that forms a club.

Pornography. Opportunities to watch pornography are ubiquitous: online, DVD, and even live. Pornography use for both masturbation and foreplay is a rational choice for many. The films' subject matter span the full range of sexual activity

BOOMERS OUT OF THE BOX

and can be ethical, erotic, and quasi-educational, or they can be violent, misogynistic, and abusive. The actors can be happy, willing participants or they could be underage, coerced, forced, drugged, or unknowing victims.

The range of sex acts depicted is all over the map and cater to almost every imaginable fantasy. But it has introduced us to many abusive, dangerous, and misogynistic practices under an illusion of normalcy. Young boys are most vulnerable to the false normal, but the rest of us are not immune to drinking the Kool-Aid. Hopefully, you will be able to tell the good from the bad as you select what might turn you and your partner on.

CHAPTER 13: SEX AND THE MODERN SENIOR

BOOMERS OUT OF THE BOX

CHAPTER 14: SEX PHYSIOLOGY 101

> *"A map says to you. Read me carefully, follow me closely, doubt me not... I am the earth in the palm of your hand."*
>
> Beryl Markham

This book is a primer and not intended to treat physiology in great depth, but we can't discuss lovemaking and orgasm without a basic familiarity with the body parts involved and some elementary instructions to get started. Many of us have not ever taken a good look at our own unique genitals. You might want to get a mirror and check yourself out if you have never done so before. See yourself as others may see you.

The intricate workings of our reproduction systems are very complex and beautifully designed to integrate male and female systems. Viewed as machines, it's like docking a space capsule with the space station. To continue the metaphor, let's identify the components and describe their functions.

THE BRAIN IS THE CONTROL CENTER

We are born with the nervous system (that includes the sensors and the "wiring") that allows the brain to work consciously and subconsciously with our "bits", as the British say when referring to sexual organs. Our brains collect data from all of our sensors, try to make sense of everything, send hormones to stimulate our organs, develop our understanding of the situation, and provide us with the capacity to act.

Early life events clearly impact our sexual development. Our attractions can be driven by the people surrounding us during our formative years and built into our value and preference systems. We are influenced by early touching experiences with other toddlers or by playing doctor in preschool years. We can form fascinations related to body parts when modesty restricts our ability to see those belonging to the people we know and love.

Fetishes may form as very young children connect to others with whom they have a strong attachment through objects such as body parts that aren't sexual organs (like feet), diapers, underwear, shoes, etc. These objects are necessary for some people to be able to experience full sexual gratification. While it may seem weird to some of us, it's neither rare nor abnormal. Adaptations of sexual activities or styles can be heavily influenced by fetishes, early porn viewing, or witnessing parental lovemaking.

> "Remember, taboos are just a map of what a society feels it's acceptable to be neurotic about. Taboos aren't rational."
>
> Comedian, Frankie Boyle

As we mature out of childhood, the brain continues to gather information from observation and experience. At the same time, our brain is processing data from our sensors with newly acquired and growing sensitivity to sexual stimulation as we respond to radical changes in hormones. Our early forays into

CHAPTER 14: SEX PHYSIOLOGY 101

sex provide feedback of all sorts that informs our brain. As our experiences expand, our exploration sends more feedback, the cycle continues. Some of us settle into a predictable pattern and quit experimenting and making changes. For others of us, experimentation becomes a life-long process.

The brain is a tremendous multitasking tool with different regions used for analyzing, prioritizing, and balancing a myriad of inputs while sending commands and responses throughout our bodies. If a person becomes aroused through thought or erogenous touch, a feedback cycle can initiate a progression that leads to great pleasure. The caveat is that if the brain is dealing with pain, nausea, grief, fear, hatred, stress, or other negative emotions, arousal loses its priority, and the process can end.

BOOMERS OUT OF THE BOX

CHAPTER 14: SEX PHYSIOLOGY 101

EROGENOUS ZONES & SEXUAL PLEASURE

There have been jokes for decades about men not knowing where the G-Spot is located. Well, it turns out many seniors of both sexes neither accurately know its whereabouts nor how to stimulate it. We can imagine that if one of the most frequently referred to erogenous zones[23] is a bit mysterious, there may be other areas that might also be under-explored.

Stay tuned, we're going to show you where it is, and how to stimulate it later in this chapter.

Figure 13. This ocean front concrete rooftop bar salutes the G-Spot. Aerial photo courtesy of Jonathan Shearer.

The stimulation of erogenous areas can be exciting in two ways, physical pleasure and mental arousal. Use of the hands,

---

[23] Areas of the body most likely to respond with arousal when touched or stimulated are called erogenous zones.

fingers, nails, lips, teeth, and tongue provides physical stimulation and mental arousal in the recipient, as well as mental arousal in the giver. Use of the penis to stimulate areas of the vulva or anus typically results in mutual physical pleasure and arousal. The joyful response to physical stimulation by the receiving partner is most often a major turn-on for the giving partner.

Passive sensors – sight, smell, taste, hearing, and receptors of touch and pressure – relay data to our control center, and our brains decide what is happening, activate the relevant emotions, and send instructions to the appropriate muscle groups to react. As they respond to arousal, any or all of the senses can contribute to the process, as can the mind even without stimulation. We are all unique, and erogenous zones differ considerably for each of us. Additionally, many of us may not know we have some of these, where to find them, nor what to do when we locate them.

While almost any area of the body can become a source of stimulation for arousal under favorable circumstances in certain individuals, the areas of our bodies with high densities of nerve endings sensitive to light touch, scratching, or tickling have the greatest potential. Many of the organs involved in the reproductive systems of both males and females become enlarged or engorged during the arousal phase. This results from blood flowing into the organs causing an increase in size, change in color, elevated firmness, heightened sensitivity, and/or erection. Mental processes of imagination and expectation, combined with physical stimulation like massage, squeezing, or pressure, as well as spanking or pain, facilitate blood flow to the strategic areas.

Organs whose sexual function requires enlargement, stretching, or expansion are triggered by arousal, but the time required from organ to organ varies. While the penis and clitoris may erect quickly, that alone does not indicate their readiness for orgasm. Vaginal areas like the G-Spot and cervix can require over 30 minutes to become fully sexually responsive.

CHAPTER 14: SEX PHYSIOLOGY 101

Many of the following erogenous zones discussed may not cause arousal in most people, but every one of them has its fans. I'd suggest spending a little time exploring all of them with your partner and/or on your own. If they are turn-ons, whoopie; if not, it's still fun to explore.

NON-GENITAL EROGENOUS AREA STIMULATION

We don't generally need to explore all of the body parts presented, but they are included here for inquiring minds and context.

Head Area

- Scalp: Full of nerve endings, and it's responsive to light touch, massage, fingernails, and in the case of baldness, kissing and licking.

- Hair: Gentle pulling and stroking can work.

- Ears: Many sensory receptors may respond to fingers, lips, and tongue action in and around the ear; even whispering or blowing lightly can be arousing for some.

- Mouth & Lips: Kissing, licking, nibbling, and sucking one another's mouth, lips, and tongue are extremely effective in building arousal in both parties:

    "It's in His Kiss"
    The Shoop Shoop Song , by Rudy Clark

- Neck: Thin skin and many nerves can respond to fingernails and kissing (sucking may be arousing, but remember it leaves a mark) from the back, behind the ears, and around to the front.

Extremities

- Inner Arms & Armpits: Soft tickling with fingertips, tongue, whiskers, or a feather can be utterly titillating.

- Inner Wrist: From light caressing to kissing to licking to passionate restraint, the wrists can be helpful in furthering the arousal.

- Hands & Fingers: Palms and fingertips are very sensitive to light finger touching; sucking fingers can be very sensual.

CHAPTER 14: SEX PHYSIOLOGY 101

- Back of Knee: Thin skinned and sensitive to licking and kissing can be enjoyable on the way to other areas or during massages.
- Bottom of Feet & Toes: Massaging feet with a full range of different pressures can increase blood flow; licking the foot and sucking on toes can stimulate some; experimentation in this area may be required to discover things that work for the couple.

Torso Plus

- Breasts:[24] The full organ is iconic and possesses the mystique of supreme sexual attraction in Western culture; it is an erogenous zone that can be stimulated by lips and/or tongue, a full hand, or fingers.
- Areola:[25] Arouse by encircling the nipple with a light touch of the finger; in the event of a supersensitive nipple, remain there.
- Nipples:[26] This classic erogenous zone can be extremely sensitive for some; sucking, licking, twisting, biting, vibrating, and clipping (using nipple clips) can bring pleasure and arousal.
- Sacrum: The small of the back immediately below the spine has many nerve endings, is surprisingly sensitive, and can respond to the slightest touch, tickle, lips, tongue or feather.
- Naval & Lower Stomach: On the path to the genitals, hands, lips, tongue, vibrator, and/or feathers can activate arousal.
- Pubic Mound: A woman's mons pubis is the fleshy mound just in front of the pubic bone and above the clitoris and has many nerve endings that are connected

---

[24] Primarily considered for female arousal, but many males respond as well.
[25] Primarily considered for female arousal, but some males respond as well.
[26] Primarily considered for female arousal, but some males respond as well.

to the genitals. Massaging the area in an up and down motion can even create clitoral stimulation. Transitioning to kissing and licking all the way to the clitoris is often effective. [14.1]

- Inner Thighs: They are highly sensitive to fingertips or by kissing and licking them directly or while kissing other erogenous areas.
- Butt Cheeks: Grasping, fondling, spanking, and massaging the butt enhances blood flow to the area and can contribute to arousal.

CHAPTER 14: SEX PHYSIOLOGY 101

GENITAL DESCRIPTION & FEMALE BIT STIMULATION

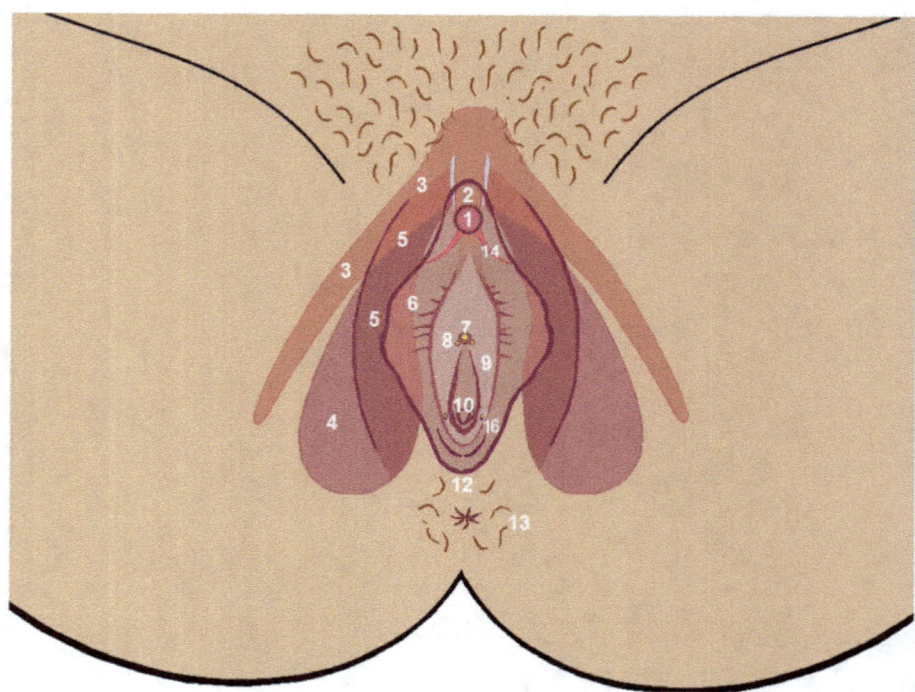

Figure 14. Vulva Exterior. [14.2]

1. Glans of Clitoris
2. Hood of Clitoris
3. Body & Crura of Clitoris
5. Labia Majora
6. Labia Minora
7. U-Spot or Urinary Meatus
8. Skene Ducts
10. Vaginal Canal or Barrel
11. A-Spot or Anterior Fornix
12. Perineal Raphe
13. Anus
15. G-Spot
19. Rectum
25. Cervix
26. Urethra

CHAPTER 14: SEX PHYSIOLOGY 101

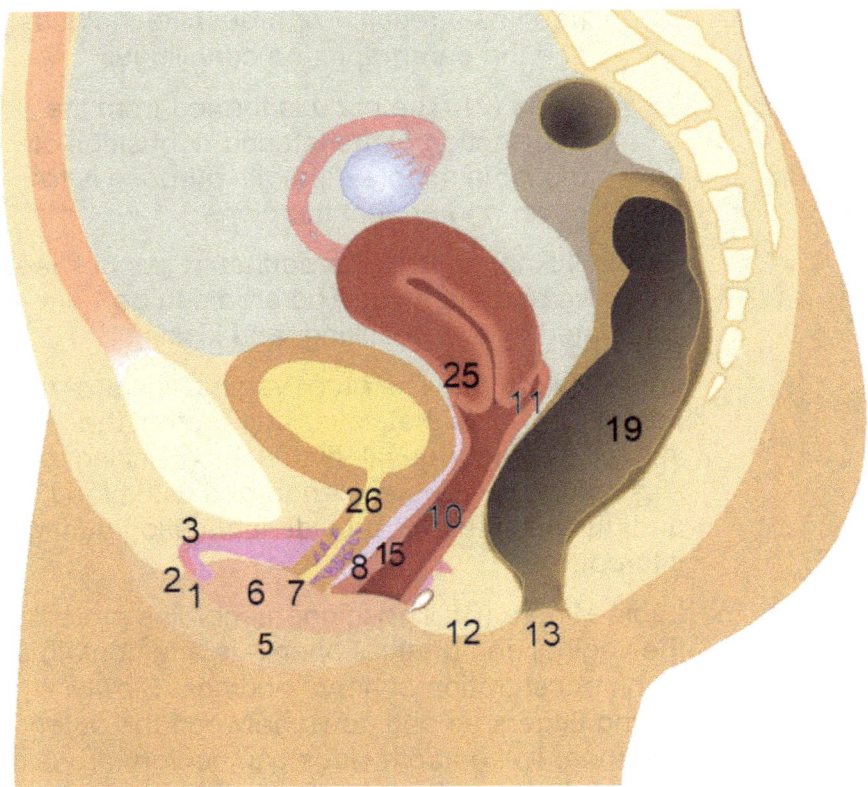

Figure 15. Lateral section of female reproductive organs. [14.3]

- Vulva: The external part of the female genitalia; stimulation of the total collection of parts at once or individually can be accomplished via hand, tongue, mouth, penis, or toy:
    - Clitoris: The primary function of this organ is pleasure, and it is the most sensitive erogenous area for most women.

199

- - - Glans (1): Typically, about the size and shape of a pea and with over 8,000 nerve endings, the glans is extremely sensitive to the point that it can easily become overstimulated and withdraw under the hood as a result. For arousal techniques, see the paragraphs on cunnilingus.
    - Hood (2): The hood is formed from the intersection of the left and right sides of the labia minora (lips); its purpose is to cover and protect the glans.
  - Perineal Raphe (12): The perineum lies between the vulva and the anus. The area can be stimulated by touch, licking, and kissing.
  - Labia Majora (5): The outer vaginal lips are a pair of fatty folds that cover and protect the vulva.[27] During arousal, by touching, licking, or kissing, the lips become engorged with blood, and gland secretions provide lubrication during intercourse.
  - Labia Minora (6): The thinner inner lips protect the vaginal and urethral openings and contain a high concentration of nerve endings. Slowly sliding fingers up and down between the outer and inner lips on both sides can be very arousing and lead the lips to swelling with blood.
  - U-Spot (7): The urethral opening (urinary meatus) has thin skin and can be stimulated lightly.
  - Skene Ducts (8): The twin openings of paraurethral ducts serve as the outlet for ejaculatory fluid.
- Vaginal Canal or barrel (10): The first couple of inches at the entrance to the vagina can provide truly

---

[27] Pubic hair helps protect the vulva from friction and mechanical stresses.

CHAPTER 14: SEX PHYSIOLOGY 101

pleasurable sensations for most women. Fingers, tongue, penis, and toys can all be used to pleasure this area. Deep penetration is pleasurable for some women as well.

- o A-Spot (11): "The A-spot is a nickname for the anterior fornix erogenous zone, an area that also has a lot of nerve endings.... It's located between the cervix and the bladder, just a few inches past the G-spot. 'The best way to stimulate the A-spot is using a longer G-spot toy. You can also go with [alternative] positions that promote deeper penetrations....'" [14.5]

- o G-Spot (15): The G-spot can be a very sensitive area for many women and stimulation of this area can even produce female ejaculation [see later in the chapter and Figure 16] in some women. *"Fingers or a curved G-spot vibrator are your best bet for reaching it. With a good amount of lube, turn your vibrator or finger upward* [in the vagina] *toward the navel and move it in a 'come hither' motion. Find what feels good and keep at it, allowing the sensation to build."* [14.6]

- o Cervix (25): *"Most women need to be fully aroused to enjoy cervical stimulation, so foreplay is a must. Any deep-penetration sex [intercourse] position can stimulate it."* [14.6] Advance with caution because impacting the cervix can be quite painful for some.

- Anus (13): *"The anus has a lot of nerve endings, which add to its popularity as an erogenous zone."* [14.5] See Anal Play later in this chapter.

Cunnilingus Techniques

Cunnilingus refers to the act of stimulation of the vulva by using the tongue and lips. As noted earlier, the clitoris is the most sensitive sex organ for most women. Not surprisingly, many women find cunnilingus one of the most enjoyable parts of lovemaking.

BOOMERS OUT OF THE BOX

Boomers, both men and women, have expressed strong positive feelings about cunnilingus. While the basic direct result is typically great physical pleasure for the woman, the general joy brought by the efforts can be a turn-on for the man as well. These examples from different individuals are indicative of many:

- [Mary] *"As I've gotten more comfortable with my body and having other people explore it, the thing that I find that brings me to a higher level of excitement is cunnilingus. It's really enjoyable to have a guy manipulate my clitoris with his tongue. It's gentler than a finger, and once I got over the embarrassment about having somebody's mouth down in that area, the feelings I got out of it were wonderful. In fact, I find that cunnilingus really helps the whole sexual experience for me."*

- [Elenor] *"I really, really, really like oral sex ... mostly with tongue and lips and kissing and sucking my clitoris or my vagina.... I find that when I squeeze my nipples at the same time, it increases the pleasure and the sensations of oral sex."*

- [Kathleen] *"...he tongues me in all the right places, on my clitoris and my inner lips. I especially like when he even sucks on my clitoris a little bit, but not too hard because if it's too much, it hurts."*

- [Elizabeth] *"I feel really tingly and excited like I'm going to burst open any minute, but I like to stay on the edge as long as possible."* [14.7]

- [Bonnie] *"I get unique lower intensity continuous orgasms when he holds his tongue against my clit and moves it very gently. It can be incredibly amazing."*

Roughly three-quarters of senior women have experienced oral sex, but not all of it was positive. Sucking or biting too roughly was an issue in some cases, but that can be ameliorated through open communication. Another inhibiting factor is fear or concern regarding vaginal odor, but one study found that the incidence of vaginal odor decreases as we age, with only 13% of women over 75 reporting odors, compared to 31% of women under 55. Here is some good-news-bad-news: many of us suffer from significant loss of smell and taste as we age.

Interviews with men also show widespread enjoyment of cunnilingus:

- [George] *"I love the sense of power I feel seeing my partner's response to my caresses."*
- [John] *"I really like to go down on a woman. I love it. I could do it for hours and hours and hours. I love the sense of pushing, of thrusting. I'd like to crawl right up through her vagina into her womb."*
- [Peter] *"I love the softness, the warmth, and the moisture, which is a direct reaction to what I'm doing, so that's terribly exciting. A woman responding to the way I touch her genitals is one of the biggest turn-ons as far as I'm concerned."*
- [David] *"She always tastes great. She doesn't douche or anything like that; there's just something special about the way she tastes and smells. I love the taste of her orgasmic fluid, too."* [14.8]

Female Ejaculation

Although most people are unaware of it, some women can and do ejaculate. Studies vary dramatically from around small percentages to over 50%, in part because many women don't know that it's occurring. Not a lot is known about the purpose of female ejaculation or how it is activated.

The ejaculate comes from the Skene's glands, also referred to as "the female prostate" and is expelled through two small holes next to the urethra. The quantity released is on the order of a teaspoon full. It typically contains some traces of urea and seminal fluid in a clear or milky liquid.

Squirting

Although often conflated and confused with female ejaculation, squirting is a gush of fluid composed of urine and water from the bladder ejected through the urethra. The squirting can occur involuntarily, but forceful massaging in the area of the G-spot with a "come hither" motion can trigger a pressured release. Some women become embarrassed or worry about messing the bed when there is a high volume of liquid.

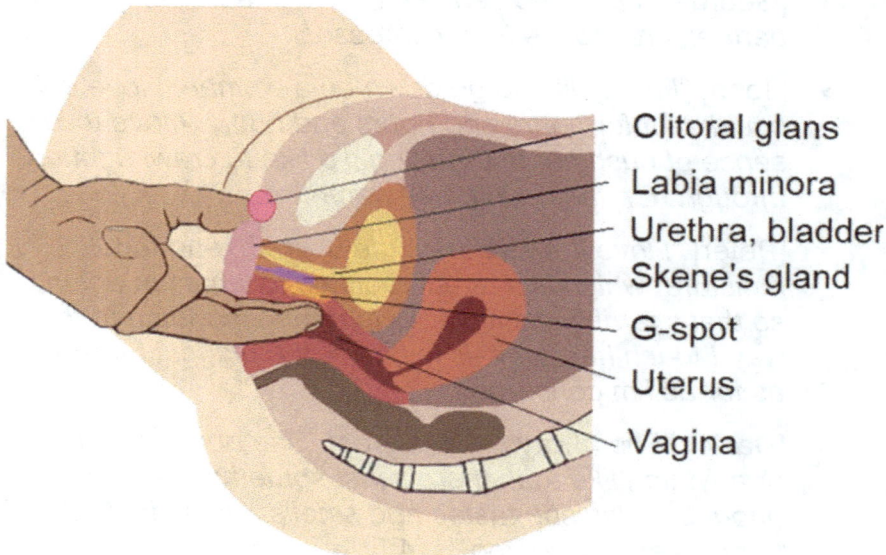

Figure 16. Manual Stimulation of the Clitoral Glans and the G-spot [simultaneously] can bring on intense orgasms. In some cases, squirting can be triggered. [14.9]

Edging

Edging is the process of building arousal close to orgasm and then slowing it down (one or more times). Doing this can result in intense sexual feelings that can lead to a more intense orgasm.

CHAPTER 14: SEX PHYSIOLOGY 101

GENITAL DESCRIPTION & MALE BIT STIMULATION

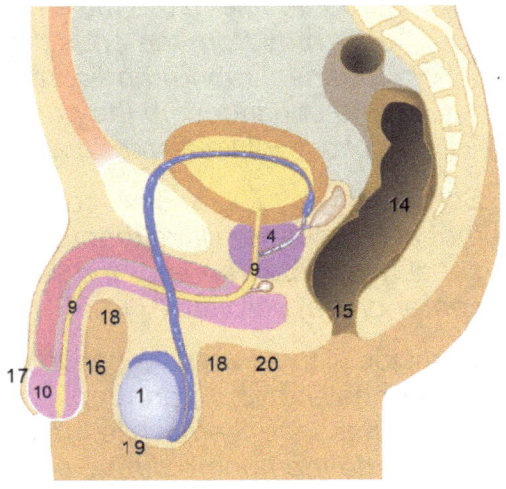

Figure 17. Lateral section of male reproductive system. [14.8]

1. Testis (Testicle)
4. Prostate
9. Urethra
10. Glans Penis or Corona
14. Rectum
15. Anus
16. Frenulum
17. Foreskin
18. Penile Raphe
19. Scrotum
20. Perineum

- Penis: The main erogenous zone for the male.
    - Glans (10): The glans penis, or corona, has roughly 4,000 nerve endings, and is the most sensitive part of the penis. See Fellatio Techniques below for stimulation suggestions.
    - Frenulum (16): *"This is the elastic piece of skin on the underside of the penis, where the shaft meets the head. It's highly sensitive and the primary trigger of orgasms in people with penises."*
    - Foreskin (17): *"The foreskin is filled with nerve endings that actually enhance pleasure for those with uncircumcised penises. This thin layer of skin provides the opportunity to mix it up for*

different sensations during a hand job or blow job."
    - Penile Raphe (18): "*The midline is part of a broader line in the male reproductive organs, that runs from the anus through the perineum (perineal raphe) and continues to the scrotum and continues up the penis to the corona, collectively referred to as median raphe.*" [14.10]
- Scrotum (19): "*The sack is composed of many nerves that are super-sensitive to touch… Focus on the highly sensitive scrotal raphe or the seam that runs down [the center of the] scrotum.*" [14.5]
- Testicles (1): "*Always be gentle when playing with your balls or having your partner play with them. You can gently massage them while masturbating or have your partner do the honors during a hand job or a blowjob.*" [14.5]
- Perineum (20): "*'…colloquially referred to as the taint or gooch, is the area between the anus and the scrotal sac. It contains fibromuscular tissue that is usually sensitive to touch, pressure, and vibrations,' …. In order to stimulate the perineum, you can try gently pushing into it with a finger or two, or you can lube up your fingers and 'glide' along it.*" [14.5]
- Anus (15): "*The anus has a lot of nerve endings, which add to its popularity as an erogenous zone.*" [14.5] See Anal Play later in this chapter.
- Prostate (4): "*This walnut-sized gland sits at the root of the penis and can lead to powerful, orgasms [when stimulated]. You can only reach the P-spot via B-town [anus], so a well-lubed finger or prostate vibrator works best. Gently insert your finger or vibrator a couple of inches into the rectum, applying pressure to the front wall. When you find the right move, keep at it. Stroke or suck the penis at the same time for maximum pleasure.*" [14.1]

Fellatio Techniques

You might start by softly passing wet lips and tongue over and around the rim of the glans of the penis. Follow this by using a lubricated hand on the shaft and taking the glans into your mouth. Next, swirl the tongue and use a hand to slide up and down gently with the thumb on the backside of the penis (frenulum). [14.1]

Most men enjoy fellatio.[28] They have, however, a wide range of how they like their penises orally stimulated.

The following notes and excerpts from extensive interviews of men identify some methods of stimulation for consideration:

- [Gene] *"I'm most aroused when my partner can create arousing friction by applying pressure to my penis with her mouth."*

- [Scott] *"The secret [to a blow job] is to use your hand as an extension of your mouth. As your mouth moves up, your hand follows, and it's all lubricated. So, it feels like the penis never leaves your mouth; your mouth and hand are like one big vagina. Then I like my partner to play with my balls with the other hand."*

- [Richard] *"I think it's much better to have her tongue wrapped around the penis and to create a little bit of suction so that the sides of her mouth are touching the penis as well. That way there's contact all the way around, and her mouth is like a little vagina."*

- [Robert] *"The underside of the penis is definitely the joy side."*

- [Eric] *"I like when my wife caresses the midline or underside of my penis with her tongue while my penis is in her mouth."*

---

[28] Many men who are experiencing erectile dysfunction may also be unknowingly suffering from peripheral neuropathy, which can significantly reduce the feeling and sensitivity in the entire genital area. This often makes the pleasure normally expected from fellatio potentially illusive no matter what technique is applied.

- [Carlos] "... I like to have a woman put two fingers at the base of the penis, one on the front side and one on the backside as she pulls the skin down, not painfully, just lightly. To me, it makes the sensations more intense. I also seem to engorge more, and my penis gets larger when that happens."
- [Peter] "I like a little bit of rough handling occasionally. It's a fine line, because it can be too rough, and it can hurt. But being overly gentle with the penis can be real boring sometimes. I have even occasionally suggested that a woman brush my penis with her teeth, very lightly...." [14.8]

While not every woman has had the experience of giving fellatio, the majority have and like it. According to women interviewed:

- [Karla] "I enjoy the sensualness of the texture and taste of my partner's penis in my mouth. It turns my partner on, and I like the sense of power and control I feel, which is a turn-on in itself."
- [Beverly] "It took me a while to be able to get over my dislike for the taste of semen. At first, it was gagging me, kind of like drinking beer, but eventually I got comfortable with it. Oral sex freed me up from simply 'lying parallel on the bed.' It makes me more active and brings a little bit of humor into sex because some of the positions we have to get into when we're trying to mutually satisfy each other can get us all tangled up."
- [Linda] "Being licked all over is a real turn-on for my boyfriend. He loves to have his balls and anal area licked and kissed and for me to stick my tongue in his anus. He likes it when I almost adore it, and he can see how I really enjoy doing it. He is particularly sensitive on the underside of his penis on down to the balls and all around the anus. He also likes me to put my finger inside his anus. I put Vaseline on my middle finger and I stick it all the way in, while I'm licking his balls. Then I move on to the penis while I've still got my finger in his

anus and I'm sucking and putting his penis all the way in my mouth. He reaches a climax pretty quickly this way so it's a real turn-on for him and for me, too."

- [Cheryl] *"I use the 'butterfly stroke,' where I flick my tongue up and down the length of the penis and back and forth over the area under the corona. And I do a lot of tantalizing stuff even before I get to the penis, like caressing the sensitive area of the upper thigh, near the crease. I go round and round the whole area with my fingers or my tongue. I do all that stroking early on and continue until he really wants me to caress his penis."* [14.7]

- [Barbara] *"My partner responds excitedly when I suck on his sensitive frenulum. He loves when I gently use my teeth on the shaft of his penis. Basically, I love giving fellatio because it's so enjoyable to watch my husband react so intensely."*

- [Nancy] *"What I enjoy most is sucking on my boyfriend's scrotum and gently putting one of his testicles in my mouth. He's told me that this is extremely pleasurable for him."*

Oral Sex

According to the Oxford University Blog:

"We analyzed 884 older heterosexual couples, with at least one spouse older than age 62, from the National Social Life, Health, and Aging Project data to provide the first nationally representative evidence linking oral sex, relationship quality, and psychological well-being. We found that receiving oral sex was positively related to both men's and women's perceptions of relationship quality, which in turn promoted their happiness and mental health and reduced psychological distress.

Interestingly, we found that men's giving oral sex was also positively related to their own emotional well-being, in part because it heightened their wife's happiness in their relationship. However, women's giving oral sex was unrelated to their own well-being although it did increase their husband's happiness in the relationship." [14.13]

BOOMERS OUT OF THE BOX

Sixty-Nine

69 is the combination of cunnilingus and fellatio typically configured with one partner on his or her back and the other on top (or both on their sides) with their heads positioned at one another's genitals. It is favored by many, but it can be mentally challenging for some to focus on what they are doing to their partner when they are being so stimulated by what their partner is doing to them. Simultaneous orgasm can sometime be experienced in this position.

Anal Play

Let's look closely at the facts.

Orlando Health Women's Institute recommends:

If you haven't had anal sex and are unsure if you want to try it, you may want to experiment with different types of anal touch to see if you find them pleasurable. One study found that 35 percent to 40 percent of women enjoyed these types of anal touch:

- *"Anal surfacing: Sexual touch by a finger, penis or sex toy on and around the anus.*
- *Anal shallowing: Penetrative touch by a finger, penis or sex toy just inside the anal opening, no deeper than a fingertip or knuckle.*
- *Anal pairing: Touch on or inside the anus that happens at the same time as other kinds of sexual touch, such as vaginal penetration or clitoral touching."* [14.11]
- Anal intercourse: Loved by some and hated by others, anal intercourse has become more popular in recent years, but it is unclear whether the rate has increased for seniors. Many find the pleasure of orgasms during anal penetration to be the most intense, but others find it too painful and/or too messy to be pleasurable.

"For anal play, you want to focus on taking it slow and have lots of lube on hand. Start by gently pushing at the [anus] with a thumb or finger and massaging around the opening. If that feels good, then you can work up to [inserting] a finger, butt

CHAPTER 14: SEX PHYSIOLOGY 101

plug, or another anal toy. 'Keep in mind the anus can stretch a lot more than people realize'. Whatever you insert into your butt should have a flared base to prevent it from being sucked inside you!" [14.5] A finger slightly inserted into the anus during other forms of stimulation can intensify the experience.

Anal sex is not without significant risks. See Chapter 15 for proper procedures and cautions.

BOOMERS OUT OF THE BOX

ORGASM: AN EXPERIENCE OF CLIMAX IN SEXUAL PLEASURE

*"Just let your love flow like a mountain stream
And let your love grow with the smallest of dreams
And let your love show and you'll know what I mean - it's the season
Let your love fly like a bird on the wing
And let your love bind you to all living things
And let your love shine and you'll know what I mean - that's the reason."*

By the Bellamy Brothers

Generally, it is the desire for pleasure and sexual climax that drives our engagement in sex acts, whether we are alone, hooking up, or sharing love with a partner. When we are fixated on orgasm, experiencing it provides a rush, but can be a bit hollow with a short half-life. This leads to a more rapid return of the need to do it again. Wonderful as orgasm is, it can be much more gratifying and sustainable when we have the presence, connection, and love of our partner in the afterglow.

Who Knew?

Over the years, there have been different theories about orgasm. Experts have differentiated types of orgasm based upon the areas that were stimulated to cause them: vaginal, clitoral, anal, nipple, etc. However, most professionals now agree that there is only one type of orgasm because an orgasm is a full-body response, regardless of the source of stimulation.

According to Medline Plus:

- *Sexual response involves the mind and body working together in a complex way. Both need to function well for an orgasm to happen.*

- *Many factors can lead to problems reaching orgasm. They include:*
    - *A history of sexual abuse or rape*
    - *Boredom in sexual activity or with the relationship*
    - *Fatigue and stress or depression*
    - *Lack of knowledge about sexual function*
    - *Lack of effective technique or a partner's lovemaking skills*
    - *Negative feelings about sex (often learned in childhood or teen years)*
    - *Shyness or embarrassment about asking for the type of touching that works best [14.12]*
    - *Differences in lovemaking styles between partners*
    - *Unrelated relationship issues*

According to The Kinsey Institute:

- *Men are more likely to orgasm when sex includes vaginal intercourse; women are more likely to orgasm when they engage in a variety of sex acts and when oral sex or vaginal intercourse is included. (NSSHB, 2010.)*

- *Women are much more likely to be nearly always or always orgasmic when alone [masturbating] than with a partner. (Davis, Blank, Hung-Yu, & Bonillas, 1996).*

- *Many women express that their most satisfying sexual experiences entail being connected to someone, rather than solely basing satisfaction on orgasm (Bridges, Lease, & Ellison, 2004).[14.6]*

According to the National Institute of Health:

"While 18.4% of women [1,055 women ages 15 to 94] reported that intercourse alone was sufficient for orgasm, 36.6% reported clitoral stimulation was necessary for orgasm during intercourse, and an additional 36% indicated that, while clitoral stimulation was not needed, their orgasms feel better if their clitoris is stimulated during intercourse." [14.14]

BOOMERS OUT OF THE BOX

In self-reported surveys, it appears that around 10% of women experience multiple orgasms during sex with a partner. It is quite rare in men. After orgasm, the penis and the clitoris both become very sensitive to touch and dissuade further activity for a refractory period. In women, that period typically varies from zero to several minutes, but for men, refractory normally can take hours or even days. Many women have experienced touching too early after an orgasm, and it can diminish desire for subsequent orgasms. If this is the case, a related discussion with your partner would be appropriate.

It will come as no surprise to women that men have always had higher rates of orgasm. Despite ED complications, about half of the men in the 70 to 80 age group self-reported having an orgasm in the previous month.

We need to acknowledge that many of the studies on orgasm lack close uniformity with other studies. The questions asked are often slightly different, and since the basis for many such studies is self-reporting, we end up with a wide variety of responses. To cull the results down to something more general, let's consider these:

- During masturbation, both men (not suffering from ED) and women orgasm almost 100 percent of the time. Note that many of those who do not orgasm give up masturbating.

- Over half of senior men suffer from some level of erectile dysfunction that prevents or curtails intercourse and interferes with the traditional way of reaching orgasm. ED alone does not necessarily prevent orgasm, but due to the lack of erection, other forms of sexual stimulation are generally required.

- During sex with a partner without ED, women orgasm two to three times more frequently during vaginal intercourse if accompanied by oral or finger stimulation of the clitoris.

Most of us have not seriously studied or read up on sex and have relied on our past experiences to guide our current sexual expectations and activities. There is a plethora of information available that can expand and refine our sexual practices, thereby increasing the pleasure we give and receive.

Satisfaction

> *"I can't get no satisfaction*
> *I can't get no satisfaction*
> *'Cause I try and I try and I try and I try*
> *I can't get no, I can't get no"*
>
> The Rolling Stones

As some of us may have experienced, the Stones could surely get as much sex as they wanted, but what may have alluded them was a close personal relationship that provided satisfaction. What is missing in the standard definition of satisfaction is duration. Orgasm and moments of extreme pleasure dissipate rapidly unless there are underlying sustainable feelings of attachment, connection, and continuity. Love provides the warmth, the afterglow, and the satisfaction in lovemaking.

Hookups and sex without emotional involvement can provide hours of exhausting pleasure, and that's not a bad thing. If the goal for the out-of-the-box senior is adventure and new acts of pleasure, the hookup and other forms of casual sex can meet expectations and provide the desired level of satisfaction. But the satisfaction the morning after may not be present if one is looking for a loving connection.

The flip side of the issue is that even with the strongest, most committed loving relationship, satisfaction may not result if the sex is lacking. "When the lovin' starts", we need to provide guidance to a partner. Without feedback, we will probably not be able to give or receive the satisfaction we seek. For seniors, the same old routines and patterns of yore are likely to prove wanting. Sex is not what it was when we were younger. Satisfaction can be elusive unless new activities and methods are employed. Open minds, experimentation, communication, and patience are required to reach nirvana.

CHAPTER 15: SAFETY

"Some of them want to use you
Some of them want to get used by you
Some of them want to abuse you
Some of them want to be abused"

Sweet Dreams (are Made of This)
By The Eurythmics
Written by Annie Lennox and Dave Stewart

SAFE SEX

Venereal Diseases

The highest rate of increase in STDs (sexually transmitted diseases) – also known as STIs (sexually transmitted infections) - is among seniors. This is often because protection is viewed as unnecessary given that many seniors think that since birth control is not a factor, no problem. The cruel surprise is that in retirement communities, some individuals have many partners, and then we all know what happens. Likewise, with online dating, which can mean having multiple partners, the results can be similar.

While no method of protection is 100% effective, condoms – male (external) and female[29] (internal) – provide reliable insurance for seniors. Dental dams (a latex or polyurethane sheet or reasonable facsimiles) provide a significant barrier for oral-vaginal and oral-anal sex. Many of the options are available at local pharmacies and online.

We can improve the odds greatly of not giving or receiving STIs when new partners provide the results of a very recent blood test for such infections or diseases.

---

[29] The FC2 Female Condom® (internal condom) is the only FDA-approved birth control option that protects against unintended pregnancy and STIs, including HIV, chlamydia, gonorrhea and trichomoniasis.

BOOMERS OUT OF THE BOX

Anal Intercourse

While anal intercourse is not for everyone, some say it can contribute to the greatest of orgasms for both men and women. If you intend to take the plunge, there are some things you need to know. First of all, the tissues in the anus are thin[30] and unprotected which renders them susceptible to tearing that can cause stinging, soreness, bleeding, and the spreading of infection. Second, the bacteria in the anal canal of one partner can infect the other. And if the penis or dildo is inserted into the vagina subsequent to being in the anus, it can result in vaginal infections and urinary tract infections (UTIs). Third, bowel movements can become irregular, difficult, or painful as a result stretching from repeated insertion of large objects (penis, fist, dildos, etc.) into the anus. Fourth, oral contact with the anus can aid the transmission of STIs from one partner to the other.

According to WebMD:

- *"The anus was designed to hold in poop. A ring-like muscle called the anal sphincter surrounds the anus and tightens after we have a bowel movement. When the muscle is tight, anal penetration can be painful and difficult.*
- *Repetitive anal sex may weaken the anal sphincter, making it difficult to hold in poop until you can get to the toilet [fecal incontinence]. Kegel exercises to strengthen the sphincter may help prevent or correct this problem.*
- *Ways to stay safe during anal sex include:*
    - *Clean well before you have sex. An enema, or anal douche, can flush you out. Make sure you ask your doctor before giving yourself an enema to be sure you're doing so safely.*
    - *If using your hands, make sure your nails are short and clean before having anal sex.*

---

[30] Anus tissue is thin and becomes thinner with age.

CHAPTER 15: SAFETY

- *After you have anal sex, change condoms before having oral or vaginal sex. You can also use a dental dam, a latex or polyurethane sheet you put between your mouth and your partner's anus.*
- *Use plenty of lubricant to reduce the risk of tissue tears. With latex condoms, always use a water-based lubricant.*
- *Relaxing beforehand can help lower the risk of tears. A warm bath may help.*
- *Stop if it's painful*
- *If you bleed afterward or you notice sores or lumps around the anus or discharge coming from it, see your doctor as soon as possible.*
- *If you're at a high risk for HIV, your doctor can prescribe a daily medication called pre-exposure prophylaxis (PrEP) to lower your chances of getting it [HIV]. You still need to use condoms to protect yourself from other STIs.*
- *If you have unprotected anal sex for any reason, you can take post-exposure prophylaxis (PEP) within 72 hours of the activity to protect yourself from HIV.*
- *Get an HPV vaccine.*
- *Afterward, clean [the anus] with mild soap and water to help prevent infection. You can also apply a water-based cream to help with soreness."* [15.1]

Planning and communication are extremely important when considering anal sex.

Check out this comprehensive article at Women's Health Magazine. [15.2]

BOOMERS OUT OF THE BOX

Choking During Sex

Sexual choking is the act of choking someone else or yourself for sexual pleasure. It falls under the umbrella of breath play. Breath play's any sex act that makes it hard for you to breathe.

Sexual choking has been both glorified and normalized through porn and mainstream films, but as presented in WebMD, it is "... *dangerous physically, mentally, and emotionally.*" [15.3] We have seen numerous accounts of police officers "choking out" suspects with various maneuvers, some with tragic results.

- Sexual choking physical side effects can include:
    - Broken facial blood vessels
    - Brain damage
    - Vocal hoarseness
    - Difficulty and/or pain when swallowing
    - Difficulty breathing
    - Tinnitus
    - Dizziness
    - Fainting
    - Loss of bladder control
    - Death
- Mental health risks:
    - Depression
    - Mood disorders
    - Memory loss
    - Degenerated mental skills

Choking and breath play during sex is always a risky activity. Even experienced BDSM professionals recommend staying away from this type of play. Nonconsensual choking during sex is both violent and illegal.

CHAPTER 15: SAFETY

Recreational Drugs

Most drugs, whether OTC, prescription, or recreational, such as marijuana, THC edibles, and cocaine, have different effects on different people. As a group, seniors respond differently from other age groups. Boomers who have been using various drugs as they have aged are likely to be more aware of the effects of the newer highly potent versions than those who are starting up again after a long hiatus. Vaping may offer good results, may be less risky, and more controllable.

According to Dr. Stahl:[31]

"There are several reasons seniors might be prone to overdose, Dr. Stall said. Many cannabis strains are far more potent than in past decades, and seniors who used the drug earlier in life may underestimate the concentrations of THC they are inhaling or ingesting. Particularly with edibles... the high can take about three hours to unfold, which might prompt users to ingest too much in the buildup.

Older adults also metabolize cannabis differently from younger people, Dr. Stall said, and their bodies eliminate the drug more slowly. Seniors also are more likely than younger people to take other medications, including psychoactive drugs for sleep, that can have problematic interactions with cannabis. And, Dr. Stall said, some seniors might already be prone to confusion or falling, which the use of cannabis could worsen." [15.5]

According to the National Institute on Drug Abuse:

Aging could possibly lead to social and physical changes that *may increase vulnerability to substance misuse. Little is known about the effects of drugs and alcohol on the aging brain. However, older adults typically metabolize substances more slowly, and their brains can be more sensitive to drugs. One study suggests that people addicted to cocaine in their youth may have an accelerated age-related decline in temporal lobe gray matter and a smaller temporal lobe*

---

[31] Matt Richtel of the New York Times wrote "Legalized Weed Is Landing More Seniors in the E.R" [15.5]

BOOMERS OUT OF THE BOX

compared to control groups who do not use cocaine. This could make them more vulnerable to adverse consequences of cocaine use as they age.

Older adults may be more likely to experience mood disorders, lung and heart problems, or memory issues. Drugs can worsen these conditions, exacerbating the negative health consequences of substance use. Additionally, the effects of some drugs—like impaired judgment, coordination, or reaction time—can result in accidents, such as falls and motor vehicle crashes. These sorts of injuries can pose a greater risk to health than in younger adults and coincide with a possible longer recovery time. [15]

CHAPTER 15: SAFETY

BOOMERS OUT OF THE BOX

BOOMERS OUT OF THE BOX

CHAPTER 16: GO FORTH AND LIVE THE LIFE YOU TRULY WANT

My purpose in writing this book is to encourage more senior singles to take action to create more fulfilling lives for themselves in these later years. As I faced singlehood unhappily at 73, I was clueless but focused, trying to figure out how to recover my joyful life. It's taken me five years to reach my goals, but I regained pieces of happiness along the way as I learned from my experiences.

HAPPINESS

More than anything, most of us just want to be happy. If we can't buy happiness, and I am certain we can't, how do we create happiness? Happiness is the result of a combination of factors that are unique to each of us. But basically, the general recipe for happiness begins with contentment and satisfaction. Mix in fun from various sources and top it off with hope for the future. But we can't expect these things to happen by themselves.

Contentment & Satisfaction

If you're thinking that your life is at a point where happiness has become impossible, here's some good news: it's more than possible – it's within your grasp. However, if you want your life to improve, you've got work to do. There are always obstacles to overcome when initiating change, and there are some things that you just won't be able to alter. If you failed to achieve previous goals in business, earnings, sports, etc., it may be too late to go back in time to amend the record, and you may need to accept the finality of history and move on. This means accepting those things you cannot change.

In the real world, we all have constraints. Your finances may not be what you had hoped they would be, so you either must come up with a plan to make improvements, or you need to accept the situation as is and resolve to live accordingly. Either way, you are likely to be a lot happier the sooner you own the situation. Get over it and make the best of it.

We all face diminished health sooner or later. You are the manager of your fitness and healthcare program. Do the best you can with what you've got and don't dwell on "shoulda, woulda, coulda …." You are also responsible for the care and feeding of your attitude; it's about the only thing in life you can fully control. Make the best of it because it can have an enormous impact on your health and happiness.

Are you afraid of things that you feel you have no control over? Mental health support may be the answer.

CHAPTER 16: GO FORTH

How's it going now?
- Do you have an active social life?
- Do you interact with friends or relatives regularly?
- Are you experiencing a high level of contentment and satisfaction with the life you are currently living?

If not, why not?
- Are you engaged in intellectual pursuits such as reading, studying, researching, writing, or teaching?
- Are you involved in arts and crafts, model building, or collecting?
- Do you participate in individual or team sports or are you involved in outdoor activities like hiking, hunting, or fishing?
- Do you enjoy bridge, poker, or other table type games?
- Are you a member of quilting, sewing, knitting, or other such groups?
- Do you volunteer for charitable causes, serve as a docent, or help in healthcare or hospice programs?
- Are you doing other things that are personally rewarding?

If not, why not?
- Are you feeling the way you want to feel?
- Are you doing the things you want to be doing?
- Are you with people who you like and love, and enjoy spending time with them?
- Do you have a romantic love life if you desire one?
- Are you missing things that you seek or need to feel good about your life?
- Do you feel fulfilled?

BOOMERS OUT OF THE BOX

If not, what's missing? What can you do about it?

Fun, Fun, Fun

Now that you're a senior citizen, have you

> "... been thinkin' that your fun is all through now?
> But you can come along with me,
> 'cause we've gotta lotta things to do now.
> And you'll have fun, fun, fun...."
>
> Fun, Fun, Fun by the Beach Boys

Are you having fun? Is fear of rejection, failure, or embarrassment holding you back from attempting something you've always wanted to do? What fun things would you like to do but aren't doing due to fear? I'm not suggesting hang gliding or any activity that risks life or limb – we take way too long to heal from major injuries at this age, if we ever do. I'm suggesting you think out-of-the-box and do things you have always wanted to do but haven't done yet. As an example:

> *I have been playing guitar and singing rock and roll since I was eight, but I only played for myself in the basement out of respect for my family and the neighbors. I always wanted to try it in front of an audience, but while the thought was exciting, I was afraid of embarrassing myself. When I was in my early sixties, my favorite bar/restaurant lost its lease and was closing, and I decided this was the perfect opportunity. If not then, when? How bad could it be? I asked the owner if I could provide the entertainment at the end-of-business party, and he thought it would be great – of course he had never heard me play.*
>
> *I put some country, early rock and roll, and some island songs together into three sets. There were little glitches, but overall, it was quite successful. Shortly thereafter, with the help of friends, we put together a band that played in bars, restaurants, and benefits for*

close to ten years. Who'd have thunk it? Sometimes you just have to jump in with both feet!

As a senior, you can push the envelope at times and even do things that are against the rules or a little bit naughty. People will often cut you slack out of deference, pity, or from their inability to stop laughing. Whatever it is, milk it. Have fun. Play strip poker, have a banana split, play Trivial Pursuit, sing karaoke, skinny dip in the pool, take a cruise, lift off in a hot air balloon, or do a million other things. The point is to fill your life with fun activities.

Tomorrow

How are you feeling about life? Are you looking forward to holidays, events, or activities on your calendar? Do you see yourself as continuing to be relevant, however you wish to define it? Do you see a meaningful role for yourself as you age?

Do you feel that you will be able to engage socially over the coming years? Are good friends nearby? Can you make new friends easily? Are you able to expand your social circle to include some younger folk?

True long-term plans may no longer make sense as our view of the horizon becomes foreshortened. However, regardless of the plans we've made or how much time we assume we might have left before the grand exit, it makes sense to live each day to the fullest. If we do that, we can't help but have a more positive attitude and a more favorable view of tomorrow, the future.

Putting It All Together

My theory is simple: contentment and satisfaction plus fun, plus hope, equals happiness. You can probably still be happy even without all of the above if you have a great attitude, but if you are not happy yet, don't give up, keep working on the parts you are missing. It ain't over 'til it's over.

BOOMERS OUT OF THE BOX

A LOVING RELATIONSHIP'S GOOD FOR YOU[32]

If you want to be happy for the rest of your life,
Avoid the perils of aging and strife.
It's my personal point of view,
A loving relationship's good for you.

If you live alone and you don't go out,
And you feel sad and sit and pout;
You'll waste your precious time away,
'til you can't play another day.

To cure loneliness and isolation,
You need to get some socialization.
It's totally tried and true,
A loving relationship's good for you.

If you start thinking outside the box,
You can make a life that truly rocks.
There's love and fun in the air,
 It's waiting for you out there.

If you think retirement means you're done,
You're going to miss out on so much fun.
If you want to find a match that's truly fine,
Romance can often be found online.

It's not the time to fear rejection,
Go out now and make a connection.
Opportunities appear left and right,
Love and fun are in plain sight.

You can do all sorts of things,
It's not over 'til the fat lady sings.
Give love the chance it's due,
A loving relationship's good for you.

---

[32] The cadence of this poem is set to that of the song, If You Wanna Be Happy for the Rest of Your Life, sung by Jimmy Soul.

CHAPTER 16: GO FORTH

DO IT AGAIN, BETTER

*"I have run
I have crawled
I have scaled these city walls
These city walls
Only to be with you
But I still haven't found what I'm looking for"*

By U2

Songwriters: Paul David Hewson / Adam Clayton / Larry Mullen / Dave Evans

We can't expect to get everything right the first time. We will make mistakes; we will have failures; and we will be rejected. Don't feel demoralized; it's part of the process. Get back the horse and do it again, only better. Practice may not make it perfect, but it can improve the results of any endeavor. Some of us will have greater challenges than others:

"My father always said, 'Be the kind they marry, not the kind they date.' So on our first date, I'd nag the guy for a new dishwasher."

Kris McGaha

While there may be no way to fix "stupid", perhaps a little self-reflection on patterns could yield some positive results for those of us in that rut. Some don't understand how they "always end up with similarly flawed (crazy, cheating, drinking, lying…whatever) partners." If this is the case, we need to recognize that we are part of the problem and seek help if we can't fix it ourselves. If we are doing the same thing over and over, we can't rationally expect different results.

One of my favorite movies is Groundhog Day. Yes, it's quite funny and internally redundant, but the high note is that it's very uplifting and gives hope to us that if we put in the time and effort, we can change, improve ourselves, and find happiness.

To make this phase of your life as fruitful as possible, it helps to remind yourself of the societal and technological changes that have occurred over the last several decades that have dramatically altered the status quo for seniors. As a group, we Boomers:

- Are living longer than our parents,
- Are much more physically fit than our predecessors,
- Are financially more comfortable than any previous generation,
- Have access to technological advances that directly or indirectly provide incredible services and opportunities formerly nonexistent, and
- Have been rebellious to the point of rationalizing and modernizing both moral and social norms, from which we now benefit.

To take full advantage of what life is currently offering, you need to have an open mind and a willingness to adapt. Adaptation is change, and in order to make change positive, doing some homework is the first order of business. This means a bit of research combined with deep thought about how you want to live out this phase of your life. What do you want to do, who do you want to become, and with whom do you wish to share this remaining time?

Change typically requires a move into the unknown because, by definition, it is not the same as what you have done before nor who you have been. There is risk in change, but many fail to realize the risk inherent in remaining the same or settling into inaction. Not changing, risks missing out on the pleasure and satisfaction gained by moving closer to grandkids, taking up a new hobby, volunteering, joining a group, finding a life partner, exploring sexuality, or a host of other possibilities.

If discovering a new love interest has been on the table, have you been effectively pursuing a new relationship? While reports show that only around 15% of online daters find long-

CHAPTER 16: GO FORTH

term partnerships, this statistic would include naïve, incompetent, and unenergetic users. Are you doing the best you can to find The One?

If your efforts have not been yielding encouraging results, you need to decide whether the dating pool is too small to find the match you are seeking, or whether your approach is falling short.

> *When I was trying to find a match while living in Puerto Rico, I determined the dating pool was way too small to find the woman I wanted. Since finding a partner was very important to me, I moved to California.*

If the pool is adequate, but the results are not, change is required. You probably need to modify your approach to find your match. More effort in finding prospects may entail using other dating sites, changing your profile and photos, or becoming more active in groups that other seniors are participating in. Either way, you have to step up and meet the challenge.

If you haven't begun, what are you waiting for? If you've been dipping your toe into the process, it's time to dive in. If not now, when?

BOOMERS OUT OF THE BOX

CHAPTER 16: GO FORTH

IN CLOSING

This book has been intended as a primer to get us started rethinking the aging process, plotting new courses, and navigating reality to new destinations. The References section includes links to a variety of areas offering more information on different topics.

Thank you for choosing to read Boomers Out of the Box. I hope that this overview has cleared some confusion, opened you up to opportunities to enjoy your life more fully, and been generally helpful.

I would sincerely appreciate feedback, questions, or any personal stories that you would like to share for future posting or publication. Please indicate if you wish to remain anonymous.

You are invited to join us at www.boomers-out-of-the-box.com to continue the journey and share our senior experiences. "Tune in and turn on", as we used to say.

Paul Lutton

paul@boomers-out-of-the-box.com

BOOMERS OUT OF THE BOX

CHAPTER 16: GO FORTH

ACKNOWLEDGEMENTS

By the time I reached the ripe old age of 78, I had met many incredible and wonderful people, learned a tremendous amount from a wide range of sources, witnessed astounding feats accomplished by others, and internalized a huge volume of information from personal experiences. Although I lived on a small island for nearly twenty years, I am not an island. I have been extremely fortunate to have been surrounded by intelligent, inspirational, and supportive friends and coworkers to whom I am eternally grateful.

This is not an acceptance speech for a Pulitzer, so I'm not thanking my mother and all the little people, although they deserve my gratitude, but I want to acknowledge the importance of those who have assisted me in the writing and publishing of this book.

First and foremost, Dr. Lonnie Barbach, Ph. D, has provided review and editing support above and beyond anything I could have ever hoped for. As a hugely successful author in her own right, her depth of knowledge and experience has been immeasurably helpful.

Taking on new projects in unchartered territory can be both intimidating and lonely. Through the consistent support and console of Jeannie McKeogh, I was able to build my confidence and persevere.

The encouragement and feedback from friends Cheri Robinson, Joy Dobson Way, Leslie Mason, and Alexa Knight were very helpful, and I truly appreciate their contributions.

BOOMERS OUT OF THE BOX

REFERENCES

1.1 Singer, Michael A. *The Untethered Soul: The Journey Beyond Yourself*, New Harbinger Publications. Inc.: Noetic Books, Institute of Noetic Sciences, 2007, page 71

1.2 IBID page 99

3.1 "Loneliness can increase the risk for dementia, a large study shows", Washington Post, Meeri Kim, Nov 14, 2024 https://www.washingtonpost.com/wellness/2024/11/14/loneliness-dementia-risk/

5.1 Tierney, John (10 April 2007). "Romantic Revulsion in the New Century: Flaw-O-Matic 2.0". Findings (column). The New York Times. https://en.wikipedia.org/wiki/Speed_dating#cite_note-7

5.2 "The Science of Flirting". Science of Love. BBC. Retrieved 1 February 2016 https://en.wikipedia.org/wiki/Speed_dating#cite_note-8

5.3 Pew Research Center, https://www.pewresearch.org/short-reads/2020/02/06/10-facts-about-americans-and-online-dating/

7.1 Achieve Healthy Aging, https://www.achievestudy.org/

7.4 "Statistics on Senior Dating" The Senior List, https://www.theseniorlist.com/senior-dating/statistics/#are-seniors-actively-dating

8.1 Smith, Dana G. The New York Times, "What New Love Does to Your Brain", https://www.nytimes.com/2024/02/13/well/mind/love-romance-brain.html

8.2 Lonnie Barbach, Ph.D. and David L. Geisinger, Ph.D., Going the Distance, Doubleday, 1991

8.3 MINDBODYGREEN, LLC, https://www.mindbodygreen.com/articles/best-dating-sites

BOOMERS OUT OF THE BOX

9.1 https://www.ncbi.nlm.nih.gov/pmc/articles/PMC3771341/#R1

9.2   Rudder, Christian, Dataclysm: Love, Sex, Race, and Identity--What Our Online Lives Tell Us about Our Offline Selves

10.1   Forbes Advisor. "Top Antivirus Software of 2024", https://www.forbes.com/advisor/l/best-antivirus-software/?utm_content=160795997977&utm_term=kwd-1556601312&utm_campaign=21329398748&utm_content=160795997977&utm_term=kwd-1556601312&utm_campaign=21329398748&gad_source=1&gclid=CjwKCAjw1emzBhB8EiwAHwZZxeyCt39RSVJwIxYGq-LaeOm_I0xunPglDnzL0CJV3EM1unRebl_OTxoCvDgQAvD_BwE

10.2   The Washington Post, "Top Antivirus Software of 2024" https://www.washingtonpost.com/technology/2024/04/23/dating-app-privacy-data/

11.1   Women's Voices for the Earth. "How Hidden Fragrance Allergens Harm Public Health" https://womensvoices.org/fragrance-ingredients/secret-scents/

12.1   Haidt, Jonathan. *The Righteous Mind.* Part 1, New York: Vintage Books,   2013

12.2   Coontz, Stephanie. The Way We Never Were: American Families and the Nostalgia Trap. Basic Books, 1992

12.3   Gray, John. *Men are from Mars, Women are from Venus.* https://www.amazon.com/Men-Mars-Women-Venus-Understanding/dp/0060574216

12.4   Pisani, Hannah. *True You Journal Article*: "Does Emotional Intelligence Depend on Gender?" https://www.truity.com/blog/does-emotional-intelligence-depend-gender

13.1   Muscle and Health. "It's all downhill from here: When is the prime of your life?", By Jack Franks, https://muscleandhealth.com/health/when-is-prime-of-life/#:~:text=In%20summary%2C%20there%20is%20no,and%20relaxed%20in%20your%2060s

REFERENCES

13.2 Mel Robbins Podcast, https://www.youtube.com/watch?v=RUPkME8y7zc

13.3 2nd Act TV, https://www.youtube.com/watch?v=dNl6-stFlDM

13.4 Are Seniors Actively Dating?" The Senior List, https://www.theseniorlist.com/senior-dating/statistics/#are-seniors-actively-dating

13.5 2nd Act TV, https://www.youtube.com/watch?v=RiNHCuQCj1w

13.6 COSMOPOLITAN, Digital Issue, "Sex After 60", https://www.cosmopolitan.com/interactive/a45947489/sex-after-60-kinsey-survey/

13.9 2nd Act TV, https://www.youtube.com/watch?v=dNl6-stFlDM

13.10 Mel Robbins Podcast, https://www.youtube.com/watch?v=RUPkME8y7zc

https://medlineplus.gov/ency/article/001953.htm#:~:text=About%2010%25%20to%2015%25%20of,for%20an%20orgasm%20to%20happen

14.1 Health Line, "Everything You Need to Know About Erogenous Zones" https://www.healthline.com/health/healthy-sex/erogenous-zones#The-bottom-line

14.2 Wikipedia https://en.wikipedia.org/wiki/Vulva

14.3 Wikipedia https://en.wikipedia.org/w/index.php?search=Lateral+section+of+female+reproductive+organs&title=Special%3ASearch&ns0=1

14.4 Cleveland Clinic. "Clítoris", https://my.clevelandclinic.org/health/body/22823-clitoris

14.5 MINDBODYGREEN LLC. "35 Erogenous Zones & Exactly How To Stimulate Them" https://www.mindbodygreen.com/articles/erogenous-zones

14.6 Kinsey Institute, Indiana University. https://kinseyinstitute.org/research/faq.php

14.7   Barbach, Dr. Lonnie and Levine, Linda. *Shared Intimacies.* Garden City, NY: Anchor Press/Doubleday,1980. Pages 65-67

14.8   Levine, Linda and Barbach, Dr. Lonnie. *The Intimate Male.* Garden City, NY: Anchor Press/Doubleday,1983. Pages 176 & 179

14.9   Manual Stimulation of the Clitoral Glans and the G-spot can bring on intense orgasms. In some cases, squirting can be triggered. Source: Pfaus, Quintana, Mac Cionnath, Parada: The whole versus the sum of the parts: toward resolving the apparent controversy of clitoral versus vaginal orgasms. In: Sociaffective Neuroscience & Psychology, 2016

14.8   Wikipedia
https://en.wikipedia.org/wiki/Male_reproductive_system

14.10   Wikipedia
https://en.wikipedia.org/wiki/Penile_raphe#:~:text=The%20penile%20raphe%20is%20part,to%20the%20female%20labia%20minora.

14.11   Orlando Health Women's Institute. "Anal Sex: What Women Need To Know", By Christine C. Greves, MD, https://www.orlandohealth.com/services-and-specialties/orlando-health-womens-institute/content-hub/anal-sex-what-women-need-to-know#:~:text=In%20addition%20to%20HIV%2C%20these,trauma%2C%20including%20pain%20and%20bleeding

14.12   Medline Plus, "Orgasmic Dysfunction In Women", https://medlineplus.gov/ency/article/001953.htm#:~:text=About%2010%25%20to%2015%25%20of,for%20an%20orgasm%20to%20happen

14.13   National Social Life, Health, and Aging Project, https://blog.oup.com/2019/02/oral-sex-older-couples/#:~:text=We%20found%20that%20receiving%20oral,health%20and%20reduced%20psychological%20distress.

14.14   National Health Institute. "Women's Experiences With Genital Touching, Sexual Pleasure, and Orgasm: Results

REFERENCES

From a U.S. Probability Sample of Women Ages 18 to 94", https://pubmed.ncbi.nlm.nih.gov/28678639/

15.1   WebMD. "Anal Sex Safety: What to Know", By Mary Anne Dunkin, https://www.webmd.com/sex/anal-sex-health-concerns

15.2   Women's Health. "How To Have Anal Sex Safely And *Still* Prioritize Pleasure", by Sabrina Talbert, Gabrielle Kassel, Mara Santilli and Zahra Barnes, https://www.womenshealthmag.com/sex-and-love/a19981443/what-anal-sex-is-actually-like-from-women-whove-tried-it/?utm_source=google&utm_medium=cpc&utm_campaign=arb_ga_whm_md_pmx_hybd_mix_us_20196160291&gad_source=1&gclid=Cj0KCQjwj9-zBhDyARIsAERjds1ZiBAxGTgKaf7ecb75WeC5YZYjsfR2M1lGiZysLEyX3tCMDUrQtaAaAhpsEALw_wcB

15.3   WebMD. "What Is Sexual Choking?", https://www.webmd.com/sex/what-is-sexual-asphyxiation

15.4   National Institute on Drug Abuse, "Substance Use in Older Adults DrugFacts" https://nida.nih.gov/publications/drugfacts/substance-use-in-older-adults-drugfacts#:~:text=Little%20is%20known%20about%20the,be%20more%20sensitive%20to%20drugs

15.5   New York Times. "Legalized Weed Is Landing More Seniors in the E.R", By Matt Richtel https://www.nytimes.com/2024/05/20/science/cannabis-seniors-poisoning.html#:~:text=There%20are%20several%20reasons%20seniors,Particularly%20with%20edibles%2C%20Dr

BOOMERS OUT OF THE BOX

LIST OF FIGURES

Cover. Collage created from modified Freepik stock photos and other free sources. https://www.freepik.com/free-photo/

Figure 1. Boomer stuck in the box. Modified image from StockCake.com.

Figure 2. Getting out of the box. Senior model Jeannie McKeogh with modified images from Freepik

Figure 3. Transition: one foot on the platform, and one foot on the train. Created from modified image at istockphoto.com

Figure 4. Is it time to change direction? Does happiness and satisfaction seem more likely on the current course or on a new one? Modified image from Freepik.com.

Figure 5. Time for a change. Opening minds may stimulate getting off the paved highway. Modified image from frimufilms - Freepik.com.

Figure 6. Enjoy the journey.

Figure 7. Loneliness is common. Socialization is extremely important for senior health. Modified image from Freepik.com.

Figure 8. Remember the soda fountain. Modified image from AdobeStock.com.

Figure 9. Getting support from our kids and grandkids for online dating. Modified image from Freepik.com.

Figure 10. Profiles.

Figure 11. Don't let a few differences ruin a match. Image by AdobeStock.com.

Figure 12. Aging may make sex a blur, but it can still be great.

Figure 13. This ocean front concrete rooftop bar salutes the G-Spot. Aerial photo courtesy of Jonathan Shearer, Vieques, Puerto Rico.

Figure 14. Vulva Exterior. Modified image from Wikipedia.com.

Figure 15. Lateral section of female reproductive organs. Modified image from Wikipedia.com.

Figure 16. Manual Stimulation of the Clitoral Glans and the G-spot can bring on intense orgasms. In some cases, squirting can be triggered. Source: Pfaus, Quintana, Mac Cionnath, Parada: The whole versus the sum of the parts: toward resolving the apparent controversy of clitoral versus vaginal orgasms. In: Sociaffective Neuroscience & Psychology, 2016

Figure 17. Lateral section of male reproductive system. Modified image from Wikipedia.com.

Figure 18. Live long & prosper. Modified image from https://www.pinterest.com.

BOOMERS OUT OF THE BOX

USEFUL LINKS

We benefit from books, speakers, and internet presentations directed at either sex so that we better understand ourselves and our potential matches. A search for relationship guidance can begin with some of the following sources:

L.1   William H. Masters and Virginia E. Johnson, <u>Human Sexual Response</u>. Preeminent authority on the physiological responses during sexual activity. The book is both technical and clinical but very informative even for lay people.
https://www.amazon.com/

L.2   Betty Dodson, Founder - artist, author, and PhD sexologist has been one of the principal voices for women's sexual pleasure and health for over four decades.
https://www.dodsonandross.com/

L.3   Erika Davian, a Men's Dating & Intimacy Coach

https://www.erikadavian.com/

L.4   2nd Act TV. Videocasts focused on the 50+ group taking charge of physical, emotional, and sexual health to live life to the fullest. With an eye towards humor, they tackle the trials and tribulations of aging head-on! Their motto: "It's never too late to be the person you always wanted to be!"
https://2ndact.tv/

L.5   National Institute of Health. Paper on sex and aging, https://order.nia.nih.gov/sites/default/files/2018-01/sexuality-in-later-life_0.pdf

L.6   Vicki Larsen, journalist and author of books on senior relationships. Her book, <u>LATitude: Living Apart Together</u>, examines the issues of avoiding cohabitation as we age.
https://www.vicki-larson.com/

L.7   Sandy Weiner, speaker, author, dating coach, offering dating and relationship courses. https://lastfirstdate.com/

L.8   Joan Price, author of <u>Naked at Our Age</u> and may others, speaker, and advocate for ageless sexuality.
https://joanprice.com/

BOOMERS OUT OF THE BOX

L.9　Michael Clayton Video on Emotional Intelligence:
https://www.youtube.com/watch?v=sHE_EgiNsTN

L.10　Joshua Freedman, Six Seconds article "What Is the Definition of Emotional Intelligence?"
https://www.6seconds.org/emotional-intelligence/

L.11　Daniel Jones, "The 36 Questions That Lead to Love"
https://www.nytimes.com/2015/01/09/style/no-37-big-wedding-or-small.html

L.12　Truth Serum, "Sex Talk with Sally"
https://www.youtube.com/watch?v=miu15mRw9vA

BOOMERS OUT OF THE BOX

ABOUT THE AUTHOR

I was born at a very early age. I grew up in Chicago, went to the US Air Force Academy and graduated with a BS in engineering, followed by an MS in Aeronautical and Astronautical Engineering from Purdue University. After that, I became an Air Force pilot and flew all over the Pacific. Upon separating from the service in 1973, I came to UC Berkeley for an MArch (Master of Architecture). In 1981 we (my wife and two sons) moved back to Chicago for family reasons, and I surfed a number of career changes, including:

- Founded a computer aided design (CAD) company selling, servicing, training, and developing custom software for the architectural, facilities management, and engineering industries.
- Became the corporate architect for a bagel franchise and designed over 400 stores.
- Opened a design-build remodeling firm focused on residential and small commercial buildings.
- Jumped on an opportunity in 2005 to pursue my dream to do residential development in the Caribbean. While living on the small island of Vieques, Puerto Rico, I practiced architecture and built houses.
- Became a full-time volunteer and board member for a nonprofit created to improve conditions on the island community after the massive destruction caused by Hurricane Maria in 2017. In this capacity, I wrote many grant requests for island infrastructure improvements, most of which were successful.

I arrived back in California in February of 2024. I'm now 78 years old and single. I dated my wife for 7 years before we married (1968) and divorced 39 years later. At 62, I was extraordinarily fortunate to meet a wonderful woman. Together we formed a joyous and loving partnership that lasted twelve years until cancer tore us apart. On and off since then, I've been attempting to find that perfect match for a long-term lover

BOOMERS OUT OF THE BOX

and partner (hopefully the same woman) using the online dating apps eharmony.com and Match.com, and by joining groups where I could meet others with similar interests. I have talked to and corresponded with many online daters who have interesting stories to share. I have been incredibly pleased with the women I have met and dated. I'm especially pleased to have found The One.

From the research, interviews, and dating experiences I've acquired, I have learned a great deal about myself and relationships. While this has certainly clarified reality and helped me to grow, I hope that sharing my insights will benefit other Boomers as they face the challenges of aging. To that end, I have begun two new services focused exclusively on seniors:

> Dating Coaching. As a coach, I can offer online and face-to-face discussion and consultation in one-on-one as well as group formats.

> Portraits. My mission is to provide photographs for senior men and women in the San Francisco Bay that will capture their personalities and natural attractiveness to enhance their ability to attract the matches they seek.

www.ingramcontent.com/pod-product-compliance
Lightning Source LLC
Chambersburg PA
CBHW072152070526
44585CB00015B/1098